Over 100 delicious recipes: Soups

DUMONT
monte

Over 100 delicious recipes:
Soups

Britta Reichel

Photography by Brigitte Sporrer
and Alena Hrbkova

General hints

Eggs If not otherwise stated, the eggs used in these recipes are of medium size.

Milk If not otherwise stated, milk used in these recipes is whole milk (3.5% fat content).

Poultry Poultry should always be cooked right through before eating. You can tell if it is done by piercing it with a skewer. If the juices run out pink, then it is not ready and must be cooked for a longer time. If the juices are clear then the bird is done.

Nuts Some of these recipes contain nuts or nut oil. People who have allergies or who tend to be allergic should avoid eating these dishes.

Herbs If not otherwise stated, these recipes call for fresh herbs. If you cannot obtain these, the amounts in the recipes can bereplaced with half the quantity of dried herbs.

The temperatures and times in these recipes are based on using a conventional oven. If you are using a fan oven, please follow the instructions provided by the manufacturer.

Contents

Introduction

According to history, the first soups were created as a result of the discovery of how to make pots, a discovery which took place 6,000 years ago in Mesopotamia, the country between the rivers Tigris and Euphrates. The art of making soup then spread to Egypt, later to Greece and from there to Rome. Travelling with the Romans, the art of making soup became an established custom wherever they made their conquests. In Central Europe, archaeologists have found soup pots made of stone and wooden plates that seem to suggest that people were eating soup here 5,000 years ago.

Old recipes reveal that the late Renaissance and the baroque age were a golden age in the art of soup making. For example: six kilos (12 lb) of beef, three kilos (6 lb) of pork, one kilo (2 lb) of mutton and a dozen pheasants, all covered with 15 litres (3 gallons) of water and simmered for 40 hours. To make it even more delicious, three or four partridges or quails could be added. After cooking, the meat was fished out and thrown away since only the soup itself was consumed, a wasteful practise that is almost unimaginable today.

The restaurant – a soup kitchen

The first eating-house serving only soup was opened in Paris in 1765 by a Monsieur Boulanger. The owner hung a sign over the entrance which said, in Latin, "Come to me when your stomach troubles you, and I will restore you". The word "restaurant" has come down to us from *restaurare*, meaning "to restore". So, according to tradition, a restaurant is really a soup kitchen!

Hot or cold

Today, soups and stews are not easy to confine to one region – they are prepared all over the world in a myriad of different flavours. Sweet, sour, peppery, hearty or delicate are just some of the adjectives that spring to mind. Usually soups are enjoyed hot, but in many countries chilled versions are common, making a particularly welcome refreshment on hot summer days. The most famous of the chilled soups are the Spanish "gazpachos", based on cucumbers, and soups made from fruit.

The traditional ways of serving soup are as varied as their preparation. In Europe they are usually served as the starter (appetizer) in a larger menu. In Asia they are a course in their own right, either between others or at the end of the meal. Whether they arrive at the table as a small snack, a first course, or a filling main course, their variety is unbeatable. They can be made from beef, poultry, game, fish or vegetables, as well as from fruit.

Soups are not fattening!

The best basis for a good soup is a home-made stock (broth) made from meat and bones, poultry, fish, herbs or vegetables. Soup has a particularly appetizing effect as a result of its flavour and the extracts of which it consists. A clear bouillon has hardly any calories, so a bowl of clear beef consommé for instance has only 18 kcal. In comparison, a slice of bread or a roll has about 85 kcal.

If the meat stock (broth) still seems to have too high a fat content, it is easy to de-grease it. Allow the soup to cool and then refrigerate it for a couple of hours. The fat floats to the top of the broth and becomes hard, so it is easy to lift off with a ladle or a spoon.

As well as the clear soups, there are the thickened or roux soups that are prepared with a base of flour. They are easily digested, and tasty vegetable soups play a major role here. Depending on the ingredients, a bowl of this kind of soup may have between 85 and 110 kcal. By adding cream or milk bound with an egg yolk, the vegetable soup advances to become a cream soup. This refinement is of course richer in calories and it may contain as many as 500 kcal per serving. But when one considers that this is the amount contained in a simple ham or cheese sandwich, then even such a "rich" soup is still a "slim" meal.

A soup becomes even richer and more filling if something is added to it. The possibilities here are even more varied than the soups themselves. Vegetables, eggs, noodles, rice or bread may be used, as well as

various kinds of dumplings. Stew is recognized as a main course in its own right. In this case, the various additions to the soup make it quite thick.

Consommé

A particularly hearty but fat-free broth – a consommé – is made by stirring 125 g/4 oz minced (ground) beef and two beaten egg whites into a broth made from 500 g/1 lb of stewing meat. Bring the soup to the boil again and allow to steep for 5 minutes. Strain through a sieve. The soup thickens nicely if a piece of chopped calf's foot is boiled up with it. It contains a lot of gelatine which thickens the soup.

Which soup should be served when?

When choosing a soup, you should always bear in mind what the main course will be. As a starter (appetizer) for a filling meal, consisting of roast beef perhaps, you should have a light soup such as egg soup rather than a heavy one like oxtail, for instance. But before a light meal, a rich vegetable cream or liver dumpling soup is quite appropriate. Gourmets like to have a fish soup as an appetizer to a fish course, but all variations of vegetable soup will work just as well in this case. In a menu consisting of several courses, a light soup is recommended. The colour and flavour should also be taken into consideration when planning a menu. It is better not to serve tomato soup before goulash, for instance, or a white garlic soup as a starter (appetizer) before a pale garlic-flavoured ragout. It would be just as unsuitable to serve a herb soup before a dish made with many herbs. You should always try to offer a variety of flavours.

Wine with the soup?

Gourmets can argue for hours about whether or not to serve wine with the soup without ever arriving at a satisfactory answer to this age-old question. But why should you not offer a glass of wine with a good bowl of soup? Nevertheless, some things should be kept in mind so as not to confuse flavours. Hearty soups such as beef or game consommé often contain a dash of

sherry. Therefore, sherry will be suitable as an aperitif and also to accompany the soup. If you are serving champagne as an aperitif, this can be drunk with the soup as well. It almost goes without saying that beer goes with a beer soup and wine with a wine soup, choosing the kind as was used to make the soup. A white wine or a rosé will go with a fish soup, as they will with any fish dish generally. Dark vegetable soups are often rounded off with red wine, and light ones with white. A light red wine is a good accompaniment to hot, spicy soups, and you can surprise your guests with a small glass of rice wine when you are serving an Asian soup.

Storage

Making a good soup takes time. Whether you are making a stock (broth) from meat or vegetables, the soup should simmer for 1½ hours over a low heat in order for the flavour to develop properly. Most soups – and this goes for almost all stews too – taste just as good, if not better, when they are reheated. When you are expecting guests, you can make the soup a day or two in advance without any problem. It will keep in the fridge for three or four days. Depending on the recipe, however, you should store any additions to the soup separately, or make them on the day it is eaten.

It is easy to freeze soups, should you want to store a larger amount. Thickened soups and additions will keep for three months, while low-fat, clear soups can be kept frozen for four to six months.

If you are planning to freeze thickened soups, you should try to reduce the amount of fat and onions you use as these may cause changes in the flavour after being frozen. When freezing, let the soup cool down, then pour into aluminium or plastic containers and freeze. To thaw, put a little water in a saucepan, add the frozen soup and heat gently while stirring the soup constantly. Check again for seasoning and add diced fried onions or butter as required.

In the case of a clear bouillon soup, it is important to de-grease it thoroughly before freezing, as otherwise it can turn rancid quite quickly. A good way of freezing soup is the space-saving way of reducing it first. To do

this, boil the unsalted and de-greased soup in an uncovered saucepan until it is reduced by half. This concentrated extract can then be poured into portion-sized plastic containers and frozen. To thaw, the frozen soup is put in a saucepan and heated gently. It is then diluted with water and seasoned with salt.

This concentrate is also a good base for sauces. Pour it into an ice-cube tray and let it to freeze for a day or two. Then hold the dish under cold, running water and press out the cubes into a freezer bag. This can be kept in the freezer without any problem. When you need some concentrate for a sauce, simply take the necessary amount of cubes out of the bag. The remainder can remain frozen.

Additions to soups

Additions to soups can be frozen in their uncooked or cooked state. Semolina or marrow dumplings can be frozen when uncooked for instance. The dough should be made according to the recipe and the dumplings then pre-frozen on a plate so that they do not stick together and lose their shape. Later they are packed into a freezer bag and deep frozen. Liver dumplings, small bread dumplings and butter dumplings should all be frozen after they are cooked. Make them according to the recipe, remove from the broth, allow to cool and freeze them on a plate to start with. Then pack the frozen dumplings in a freezer bag.

To thaw, simply add the frozen additions to the soup, allow the uncooked ones to cook in the hot soup before serving.

Ready-made products

For those who do not have a lot of time to cook or do not have a deep freeze, there are many ready-made products available in the supermarket. The selection is enormous. It ranges from instant vegetable or meat stock (broth) cubes through liquid concentrates in a jar, to ready-to-eat soups in tins or packages. If you want to add your own touch to a tinned soup, you can season it with some cream or a dash of sherry and it will taste nice, but it will never achieve the flavour of a home-made soup. There are ready-made essences in all flavours, fish or game for instance. The disadvantage is that once opened they have must be used up quite quickly. Among the instant products, vegetable stock (broth) powder from health food shops and some supermarkets is to be recommended, since it does not contain any monosodium glutamate.

The instant stock (broth) cube has largely won the battle against the home-made variety long ago. The quality of the extract from beef or chicken, or from vegetables, and the flavour they retain is now so good that only a gourmet can really tell the difference.

The selection of vegetables in the freezer section of the supermarket is also so full of variety that vegetable soups, cream soups or stews can be made just as easily with them as with fresh vegetables.

Soak pulses in hot water, not cold

Pulses such as lentils, dried beans, peas and chick peas (garbanzo beans) are extremely healthy and they are very popular in soups and stews. However, dried pulses need long cooking and should be soaked in water overnight. You can shorten the soaking time if you soak them in hot water instead of cold, as follows. first wash the pulses and put them in a saucepan. Add double the amount of water. Heat the saucepan slowly on the stove but do not let it boil; if it gets too hot, the beans or lentils will become hard. Cover the saucepan and wrap up in cloths, or leave it on a *very* low heat on the stove. After about four hours, you can start the preparation of your meal.

Everything depends on the saucepan

By using a pressure cooker you can reduce the cooking time of your soups and stews considerably. Some experts vehemently reject this device. But if you are in a hurry and need to make a meal appear on the table in less than an hour, you will appreciate its advantages. When things have to happen quickly, a pressure cooker is a sensible tool. Making meat stock (broth) takes only 20 minutes instead of 2 hours and a lentil stew only 10 minutes instead of a good hour. But be sure to read

saucepans conduct heat very well and are therefore very suitable for cooking stews. They are also attractive and the soup can be served directly from them. They also keep the food hot for a long time. But a cast-iron saucepan is very heavy, and it rusts easily. After being washed, it must always be dried carefully before being put away in the cupboard. As an alternative there are enamelled cast-iron pots and pans.

When buying a saucepan, you should pay particular attention to the heat conductivity of the base of the saucepan. It is this that determines how fast a soup can be brought to the boil. In the case of stoves with glass ceramic cooking surfaces, it is essential that the base of the saucepan should be absolutely flat so that it can pick up the heat directly. Whatever the kind of heat, the base of the saucepan should never be smaller than the heat source, as this is a great waste of energy.

Useful appliances

When making cream or vegetable soups, a hand-held blender is very useful. This saves yourself the trouble of pressing everything through a sieve. If you do not have a hand-held one then you can purée your soups in a normal blender. If the soup only needs to be roughly puréed, then a potato masher will also do the trick.

the instructions carefully beforehand. Never cook for longer than the times stipulated or the ingredients will become overcooked and soft. It is not just the cooking time that is reduced; the energy used for cooking is reduced by 50 percent. This is because the heat can be lowered to a minimum once the correct temperature has been reached.

If you decide to buy a pressure cooker, be sure not to purchase one that is too small. Soups in particular can be cooked and stored, so the cooker should be able to hold a double quantity.

People with a little more time can make soups in stainless steel saucepans. As steel is not a very good conductor of heat, you should buy pans with thick aluminium or copper bottoms. Cast-iron casseroles and

Basic recipes

The infinite variety of soups and their flavours is one of their great attractions. Nonetheless, they are based on a fairly small number of basic recipes. Here are basic recipes for stocks (broths) using meat (page 22), vegetables (page 21), chicken (page 25) and fish (page 28). These are the foundation of many of the recipes in this book, and with them you will also be able to create a wide variety of your own soups, limited only by your imagination.

White roux soup

This is the basis for many delicate soups and can be combined with vegetables, herbs and spices to taste. Soups made with starch often thicken up again later, so it is a good idea to test the consistency before serving and dilute it a little if necessary.

50 g/2 oz (¼ cup) butter

50 g/2 oz (½ cup) white flour

1 litre/1¾ pints (4½ cups) meat, fish or vegetable stock (broth)

❶ Heat the butter until it sizzles but do not let it become brown. Add the flour and beat until smooth. Cook over gentle heat.

❷ Add the liquid gradually, beating to keep it smooth.

❸ Simmer the soup for about 20 minutes so that the taste of uncooked flour is no longer present.

Serves 4. About 200 kcal per serving

Brown roux soup

A little more flour is needed for the brown roux, since the flour's thickening capacity is reduced by being browned. 100 g (3½ oz) of finely diced vegetables can be sautéed in the butter. They must be taken out before adding the flour but they may be returned when the liquid is added.

50 g/2 oz (¼ cup) butter

70 g/3 oz (¾ cup) white flour

1 litre/1¾ pints (4½ cups) meat stock (broth)

❶ Melt the butter in a pan and allow to become light brown. Add the flour and beat until smooth. Sweat gently over medium heat until brown.

❷ Gradually add the liquid, beating to keep it smooth.

❸ Simmer the soup for about 20 minutes so that the flour loses its uncooked taste.

Serves 4. About 220 kcal per serving

Vegetable stock (broth)

This vegetarian version of bouillon is the basis for many meals. Other vegetables can be used in addition to the ones mentioned in this recipe. The amounts can also be varied. It is easy to blend the cooked vegetables to a purée with cream.

❶ Wash the vegetables. Depending on the variety, dice, cut into rings or separate into florets.

❷ Put the prepared vegetables, herbs and spices into a large saucepan and cover with cold water.

❸ Simmer the broth uncovered for about 40 minutes, skimming from time to time as necessary. Strain through a sieve and use the vegetables for another recipe.

Serves 4. About 15 kcal per serving

½ **small savoy cabbage or green cabbage**

1 **kohlrabi**

4 **large carrots**

2 **leeks**

½ **celeriac**

3 **sticks (stalks) celery**

¼ **cauliflower or 1 head of broccoli**

1 **onion**

3 **cloves garlic**

½ **bunch parsley**

2 **sprigs thyme**

1 **bay leaf**

1 **teaspoon black peppercorns**

salt

Beef stock (broth)

Good beef stock (broth) is the foundation for many soups with vegetables, noodles or eggs added to it. It is also the basis for various kinds of thickened soups. The browned onions give it a nice, golden colour. Do not boil the stock (broth) with the lid on, or it will become cloudy.

1 kg/2 lb well-marbled beef

3 beef marrowbones

1 carrot

1 slice celeriac

1 small leek

1 onion

2 cloves

1 bay leaf

1 teaspoon black peppercorns

❶ Wash the meat and bones under cold running water and put in a tall large saucepan. Wash and dice the vegetables and add them to the pan.

❷ Halve the onions without peeling them and brown the cut surfaces in a dry frying pan over medium heat. Push the cloves into the onions and put them and the rest of the spices in the saucepan.

❸ Cover with cold water and bring slowly to the boil. Skim the surface repeatedly.

❹ Simmer the broth without a lid for at least 1½ hours. Line a sieve with cheesecloth, remove the meat from the saucepan and strain the stock (broth) through the sieve. De-grease if necessary before using it.

Serves 4. About 145 kcal per serving

Chicken stock (broth)

A real boiling fowl has much more flavour than its more tender cousin, the roasting chicken. However, once it is boiled, the meat is no longer a delicacy. It is best to use it for a fricassee with a creamy sauce.

❶ Wash the chicken under cold, running water and cut off and discard the parson's nose. Put the chicken in a large saucepan and cover with cold water.

❷ Halve the unpeeled onions, brown the cut surfaces in a dry frying pan and stud with the cloves. Wash and chop up the remaining vegetables and add to the chicken with the onions, herbs and spices. Add salt only sparingly.

❸ Simmer the stock (broth) gently for 1½ to 2 hours without a lid and skim repeatedly. Remove the chicken and use for another dish. Strain the stock (broth) through a sieve. If necessary, remove the fat before using further.

Serves 4. About 110 kcal per serving

1 large boiling fowl

1 small onion

1 carrot

¼ celeriac

1 leek

1 parsnip

½ bunch parsley

1 sprig thyme

1 bay leaf

2 cloves

1 teaspoon black peppercorns

salt

Classic meat bouillon

This tasty bouillon becomes a hearty meat dinner if you add 250 g/8 oz of lean minced (ground) beef to the finished bouillon, bring it to the boil and simmering it for half an hour before straining through a sieve. This broth can be cooked in large amounts since it freezes well.

❶ Wash the meat and bones in cold water and put into large saucepan. Cover with cold water and bring to the boil. Skim repeatedly.

❷ Wash the vegetables, cut lengthways and tie into a bundle with the herbs. Push the cloves into the unpeeled onion and put everything in the pan with the remaining spices.

❸ Simmer without a lid for about three hours. Remove the meat and strain the stock (broth) through a sieve. If necessary, de-grease before using further.

Serves 4. About 145 kcal per serving

1 kg/2 lb stewing beef

3 shin bones

1 chicken carcass

2 large carrots

1 leek

1 parsnip

1 stick (stalk) celery

2 cloves garlic

1 unpeeled onion

2 cloves

1 bay leaf

1 teaspoon black peppercorns

salt

Game stock (broth)

Meat and bones are often left over when cooking game which it would be a pity to throw away. They can be used to make a wonderful soup.

❶ Pre-heat the oven to 220°C (425°F), Gas Mark 7. Butter a large roasting tin, put in the bones and leftover meat and roast for 25 minutes. Stir occasionally, since the bones should be browned on all sides if possible.

❷ Meanwhile, wash the parsnips, celeriac, carrots and shallots and cut them into large chunks. After 20 minutes add them to the bones and meat and roast them also.

❸ Take the roasting tin out of the oven and put the contents in a large saucepan. Add the thyme, juniper berries, cloves, bay leaf and peppercorns. Pour over the red wine and vegetable stock (broth) and bring to the boil on the top of the cooker.

❹ Skim as soon as the stock (broth) starts to boil and simmer for 1½ hours. Strain the broth through a clean, tightly woven tea towel.

❺ Add sherry, salt and freshly ground pepper to taste. Allow the stock (broth) to cool, de-grease and then bring briefly to the boil once again. Serve in small soup bowls and garnish with chopped chives.

Serves 4. About 60 kcal per serving

1 tablespoon butter

500 g/1 lb bones and leftover trimmings from venison or hare (have the butcher cut them up for you)

1 parsnip

1 celeriac weighing 150 g/5 oz

1 carrot

2 shallots

1 sprig fresh thyme

4 juniper berries

2 cloves

1 bay leaf

5 black peppercorns

750 ml/1¼ pints (3½ cups) dry red wine

1 litre/1¾ pints (4½ cups) vegetable stock (broth)

a dash of sherry

salt

fresh-ground black pepper

2 tablespoons chopped chives

Fish stock (broth)

Making your own fish stock (broth) may be more trouble than opening a tin, but as an important ingredient of soups and sauces it is much better and more delicious. Reduced, fish stock (broth) can be frozen and stored in small quantities. so that this little taste sensation is ready to hand whenever you need it.

1 kg/2 lb fish heads and bones (from the fishmonger's)

2 shallots, peeled and cut into quarters

1 leek

½ fennel bulb

1 parsnip

1 stick (stalk) celery

50 g/2 oz (4 tablespoons) butter

250 ml/8 fl oz (1 cup) dry white wine

2 litre/3½ pints (9 cups) water

1 bay leaf

3 sprigs thyme

1 teaspoon white peppercorns

❶ Remove the gills from the fish heads (they give the stock (broth) a bitter taste), cut up the fish pieces, wash thoroughly and drain well.

❷ Wash the vegetables and cut into chunks. Heat the butter in a large pan until it sizzles and fry the fish pieces over medium heat without letting them become brown.

❸ Add the vegetables and sauté briefly. Add the wine, water and spices. Bring slowly to the boil over a low heat, skimming frequently.

❹ Simmer the stock (broth) for 20 to 30 minutes, then strain through a sieve lined with cheesecloth.

Serves 8. About 70 kcal per serving

Herb and vegetable soups

There is hardly a vegetable to be found that cannot be used to make a tasty soup. The wide variety of vegetables makes it easy to find the right ones for your soup. You can also make delicious soups from the herbs and plants growing in your garden or growing wild in unsprayed fields. Try the watercress soup (page 37) or the sorrel soup (page 40).

Rocambole garlic soup

Rocambole, a plant of the allium family, is cultivated in parts of France, and elsewhere the strong-smelling leaves of wild garlic can be gathered in the woods to make this savoury soup. It can sometimes be bought from market stalls. White bread croutons fried in butter go well with it.

120 g/4 oz rocambole garlic leaves

750 ml/1¼ pints (3½ cups) chicken stock (broth)

2 small onions

2 tablespoons butter

2 tablespoons cornflour (corn starch)

100 g/3½ oz crème fraîche

salt

freshly ground black pepper

❶ Wash the rocambole, pick it over and dry it. Cut into fine strips. Set some aside as a garnish for the soup and cook the rest in 250 ml/8 fl oz (1 cup) chicken stock (broth) for 5 minutes. Strain through a sieve and return the cooking liquid to the rest of the stock (broth).

❷ Peel the onions, dice finely and sweat in the heated butter. Add the cooked strips of rocambole and sauté briefly.

❸ Add the rest of the stock (broth). Beat the cornflour (corn starch) to a smooth paste with some cold water and stir it into the stock (broth). Simmer for five minutes.

❹ Stir in the crème fraîche. Season with salt and pepper.

❺ Garnish with the reserved strips of rocambole and serve.

Serves 4. About 220 kcal per serving

Rocambole garlic cream soup

Spring is the season for rocambole or wild garlic, and wonderful aromatic dishes can be prepared with it. The long sickle-shaped leaves may be found under spreading trees or on the banks of shady streams. Sometimes it can also be bought in street markets.

❶ Wash the spring onions (scallions) and cut into fine rings. Peel the potatoes and cut them into eighths. Melt the butter in a saucepan and sauté the onions and the potatoes for 5 minutes.

❷ Add the vegetable stock (broth) and allow to simmer for 20 to 25 minutes. Purée the soup, stir in the cream and briefly bring to the boil again.

❸ Wash the rocambole, chop it finely and stir it into the soup. Season with salt and freshly ground pepper.

Serves 4. About 240 kcal per serving

3 spring onions (scallions)

3 medium potatoes

2 tablespoons butter

750 ml/1¼ pints (3½ cups) vegetable stock (broth)

250 ml/8 fl oz (1 cup) cream

50 g/2 oz rocambole leaves

salt

freshly ground pepper

Nettle soup

Young nettles have a subtle, bitter taste and are rich in vitamins. They are also kind to the budget, since you have to pick them yourself. As with spinach, nettles can also be used as a vegetable or a salad.

8 handfuls of young nettles

750 ml/1¼ pints (3½ cups) beef stock (broth)

2 shallots

1 clove garlic

2 tablespoons butter

2 tablespoons plain (all purpose) flour

250 ml/8 fl oz (1 cup) milk

2 boiled potatoes

1 tablespoon oil

salt

freshly ground pepper

2 tablespoons sour cream

❶ Wash the nettles and pick them over. Simmer with the stock (broth) for 7 minutes. Strain through a sieve and set aside the cooking liquid.

❷ Peel the shallots and garlic and chop finely. Sweat in the butter until they become transparent. Dust with flour, sweat briefly and slowly stir in the milk with a balloon whisk.

❸ Add the cooking water from the nettles and simmer for 15 minutes.

❹ Meanwhile, peel and dice the potatoes. Fry in hot oil until golden brown.

❺ Add the nettles to the soup and purée it. Add salt and pepper to taste.

❻ Ladle the soup into bowls. Garnish with the fried, diced potatoes and a swirl of sour cream.

Serves 4. About 240 kcal per serving

Watercress soup

Watercress is appreciated for its piquant taste and its high iron content. You can also make this soup with garden cress. The addition of poached oysters turns this soup into a luxurious first course.

❶ Wash and pick over the watercress, dry and chop coarsely.

❷ Heat the stock (broth) and milk together in a saucepan. Mix the cornflour (corn starch) to a smooth paste with a little cold water and add it to the saucepan using a balloon whisk. Allow to simmer for 5 minutes. Add lemon juice, salt and pepper to taste.

❸ Mix the cream with the egg yolks. Peel the hard-boiled (hard-cooked) eggs and chop them finely.

❹ Remove the soup from the heat and thicken with the egg and cream mixture.

❺ Put the chopped watercress in soup plates, ladle the soup over it and serve garnished with the chopped egg.

Serves 4. About 230 kcal per serving

1 bunch watercress

750 ml/1¼ pints (3½ cups) beef stock (broth)

250 ml/8 fl oz (1 cup) milk

2 level tablespoons cornflour (corn starch)

juice of ½ lemon

salt

freshly ground white pepper

100 ml/3½ fl oz (½ cup) cream

2 egg yolks

2 hard-boiled (hard-cooked) eggs

Chervil soup

Chervil soup is traditionally eaten in Bavaria on Maundy Thursday. It should always be made using fresh chervil and can be refined with cream or crème fraîche.

❶ Wash the spring onions (scallions) and cut into fine rings. Heat the butter in a large saucepan and sweat the onions. Dust with the cornflower (corn starch) and brown for several minutes.

❷ Add the vegetable stock (broth), beat with a balloon whisk and simmer for 30 minutes. Wash the chervil, setting a few sprigs aside for the garnish. Remove the stalks from the remaining sprigs and chop fine.

❸ Add the chervil to the soup, simmer for 10 minutes, then stir in the cream or crème fraîche as desired. Keep the soup warm but be careful not to boil it again.

❹ Add salt and pepper to taste, ladle into soup bowls and garnish with the sprigs of chervil.

Serves 4. About 230 kcal per serving

2 spring onions (scallions)

50 g/2 oz (4 tablespoons) butter

2 tablespoons cornflour (corn starch)

1 litre/1¾ pints (4½ cups) vegetable stock (broth)

1 large bunch chervil

salt

freshly ground white pepper

if desired, 100 ml/3½ fl oz (½ cup) cream or 2 tablespoons crème fraîche

Herb cream soup

The herbs that are available at the time will determine which ones used for this soup. There should be at least four different kinds, so that the soup is really aromatic. The basis is a delicate chicken stock (broth), refined with cream towards the end of the cooking time.

❶ Wash the herbs, dry them with a tea towel and remove the stalks. Chop finely on a large board and sprinkle with lemon juice.

❷ Clean the spring onions (scallions) and cut into fine rings. Heat the butter in a saucepan and sauté the onions. Dust with cornflour (corn starch) and add the chicken stock (broth), stirring carefully to avoid lumps.

❸ Add the white wine and cream and simmer for a few minutes. Add the chopped herbs and leave to steep for 5 minutes, but be careful not to boil it again.

❹ Season the soup with salt, pepper and grated nutmeg and serve with croutons.

Serves 4. About 180 kcal per serving

Total of 150 g/6 oz fresh herbs (for instance, chervil, tarragon, parsley, chives, sorrel, dill, watercress or lemon balm)

1 tablespoon lemon juice

3 spring onions (scallions)

1 tablespoon butter

1 tablespoon cornflour (corn starch)

500 ml/17 fl oz (2¼ cups) chicken stock (broth)

125 ml/4 fl oz (½ cup) white wine

125 ml/4 fl oz (½ cup) cream

salt

pepper

nutmeg

Sorrel soup

You can pick this wild-growing herb with its slightly bitter taste yourself in the spring, or it can sometimes be bought from the greengrocer. This recipe makes an excellent sauce for fish if only half the quantity of liquid is used.

250 g/8 oz sorrel

25 g butter

100 ml/3½ fl oz (½ cup) dry white wine

500 ml/17 fl oz (2¼ cups) veal stock (broth) (ready-made)

2 boiled potatoes, peeled

100 g/3½ oz crème fraîche

freshly ground white pepper

salt

❶ Wash and pick over the sorrel. Dry it and cut into fine strips.

❷ Melt the butter in a saucepan. Add two-thirds of the sorrel, all the wine and the veal stock (broth) and simmer for 7 minutes. Dice the potatoes and add to the soup. Purée the soup and pass it through a sieve.

❸ Stir the crème fraîche into the soup, adding salt and pepper to taste. Re-heat the soup briefly and garnish with the remaining strips of sorrel.

Serves 4. About 230 kcal per serving

Spinach cream soup

You only need a few ingredients for this delicious cream soup. The pine kernels give the soup the necessary extra something and you can be certain it will be praised by your guests.

1 tablespoon butter

2 shallots

300 g/10 oz fresh spinach

750 ml/1¼ pints (3½ cups) vegetable stock (broth)

1 large floury potato

nutmeg

salt

freshly ground white pepper

100 g/3½ oz crème fraîche

50 g/2 oz (⅜ cup) pine kernels

❶ Heat the butter in a large saucepan. Peel and chop the shallots, then sweat in the butter until transparent. Wash the spinach and add to the shallots. Steam until the spinach collapses slightly.

❷ Add the vegetable stock (broth). Peel the potato and cut into small dice. Add to the soup and simmer for 10 to 15 minutes with the lid on, until the potatoes are done.

❸ Purée the soup and season with grated nutmeg, salt and pepper. Over a very low heat, fold in the crème fraîche. Do not let the soup boil again.

❹ Ladle the soup into bowls, chop the pine kernels and sprinkle them over it. Serve with fresh white bread.

Serves 4. About 250 kcal per serving

Leek soup with saffron

This soup combines two interesting aromas and is very striking with the glowing orange-yellow of the saffron. Adding one or two king prawns (shrimps) to each serving makes this soup fit for a party menu.

❶ Wash the leeks and cut the white and light green parts (only) into rings. Peel and dice the potatoes.

❷ Blanch one-third of the leek rings in boiling salted water until just done and plunge into cold water. Drain in a colander. Peel and crush the garlic.

❸ Heat the oil in a saucepan and sweat the rest of the leek with the potatoes and garlic, but do not let them brown. Add the stock (broth) and simmer for 20 minutes.

❹ Meanwhile, make the saffron sauce. Heat the butter until it begins to sizzle in a small pan. Add the blanched leek and the saffron strands, and pour in 4 tablespoons of water.

❺ Purée the soup. Stir in the crème fraîche and add salt, pepper and freshly grated nutmeg to taste.

❻ Ladle the soup into warmed soup plates, garnish with the leek rings and a swirl of the saffron sauce.

Serves 4. About 240 kcal per serving

2 large leeks
250 g/8 oz floury potatoes
salt
1 clove of garlic
2 tablespoons oil
750 ml/1¼ pints (3½ cups) beef stock (broth)
30 g/1 oz (2 tablespoons) butter
½ teaspoon saffron strands
2 tablespoons crème fraîche
salt
freshly ground white pepper
nutmeg

Pea soup

Many people associate pea soup with winter weather and skiing, and indeed this nutritious soup is normally best in cold weather. It becomes a more summery dish if one leaves out the pork and the potatoes and serves the puréed soup with cream and fresh mint leaves.

200 g/7 oz (1¾ cups) dried peas

1 onion

1 carrot

1 parsnip

1 leek

2 floury potatoes

2 tablespoons oil

2 litre/3½ pints (9 cups) stock (broth)

200 g/7 oz belly of pork (1 slice)

1 bay leaf

salt

freshly ground white pepper

1 pinch ground allspice

2 tablespoons chopped parsley

❶ Soak the peas overnight in 1 litre/1¾ pints (4½ cups) of water. Wash the vegetables, cut the leek into rings and dice the rest.

❷ Heat the oil in a saucepan and sweat the vegetables. Strain the peas, add to the pan and fill up with the stock (broth). Put in the pork and bay leaf and simmer everything on a low heat for 2 hours.

❸ Take the pork out of the soup, cut off the rind, dice the meat and return it to the soup.

❹ Season with salt, pepper and allspice and serve sprinkled with parsley.

Serves 4. About 340 kcal per serving

Carrot cream soup

Delicately mild and faintly sweet in flavour, this cream of carrot soup with potatoes is a real delight for the palate. When rounded off with crème fraîche, the aroma of the soup unfolds itself to perfection.

❶ Melt the butter in a large saucepan. Peel and chop the shallots, then sweat in the butter until transparent.

❷ Peel and dice the carrots and potatoes, add to the shallots and sweat them too. Add the vegetable stock (broth) and the milk and simmer for 20 minutes on a gentle heat with the lid on.

❸ Remove the soup from the heat, purée it and stir in the crème fraîche. If the soup is too thick, add a little more milk and bring to the boil again. Add salt, pepper, some grated nutmeg and the orange juice to taste.

❹ Wash the parsley, remove the stalks and chop it finely. Ladle the soup into soup plates, sprinkle over the parsley and serve with the croutons.

Serves 4. About 270 kcal per serving

2 tablespoons butter

2 shallots

500 g/1 lb carrots

200 g/7 oz floury potatoes

750 ml/1¼ pints (3½ cups) vegetable stock (broth)

250 ml/8 fl oz (1 cup) milk

125 g/4 oz crème fraîche

salt

freshly ground white pepper

nutmeg

juice of 1 orange

1 bunch flat-leaf parsley

croutons

Classic tomato soup

Tomato soup is always good as a starter (appetizer) for a large menu since it is light and appetizing and goes well with many dishes. The pinch of sugar is an important part of the recipe.

❶ Peel and dice the shallots. Clean the spring onion (scallion) and cut into fine rings. Heat the olive oil in a saucepan and sweat the vegetables.

❷ Wash the tomatoes, cut into quarters and remove seeds. Add to the pan and cook for 3 minutes. Reserving 2 tablespoons of the stock (broth), add the rest to the tomatoes and simmer everything over a low heat for 20 minutes. Pass the tomato soup through a fine sieve.

❸ Heat the butter in small pan, carefully beat in the cornflour (corn starch) and the rest of the stock (broth), then beat it into the tomato soup. Be careful that no lumps appear.

❹ Season the soup with salt, pepper and a pinch of sugar. Ladle into four soup plates, add a spoonful of crème fraîche to each and sprinkle the finely chopped parsley over the top.

Serves 4. About 170 kcal per serving

2 shallots

1 spring onion (scallion)

2 tablespoons olive oil

500 g/1 lb ripe tomatoes

750 ml/1¼ pints (3½ cups) vegetable stock (broth)

2 tablespoons butter

1 tablespoon cornflour (corn starch)

salt

pepper

sugar

4 teaspoons crème fraîche

1 tablespoon chopped parsley

Avocado cream soup

This avocado soup is served hot and should be accompanied by toasted bread. As avocados are very rich, this soup makes a light meal in itself.

❶ Halve the avocados, remove the stone (pit), peel and cut the flesh into chunks. Sprinkle immediately with lemon juice to stop them turning brown.

❷ Mash the pieces of avocado with a fork and purée them. Put in a saucepan and gradually add the vegetable stock (broth) and white wine, stirring in well. Only add enough liquid to give the soup a creamy consistency.

❸ Season the avocado cream with salt and pepper and add the crème fraîche. Bring briefly to the boil. Ladle into soup bowls and serve with croutons as desired.

Serves 4. About 270 kcal per serving

2 ripe avocados

juice of 1 lemon

750 ml/1¼ pints (3½ cups) vegetable stock (broth)

125 ml/4 fl oz (½ cup) dry white wine

salt

freshly ground white pepper

125 g/4 oz crème fraîche

Green asparagus soup

With this recipe you can make a delicious cream soup with just a few ingredients. During the asparagus season it can be the highlight of every meal. Green asparagus plays the main role and a large amount of fresh parsley is needed to round the soup off to perfection.

❶ Wash the green asparagus and cut off the stringy ends. Peel only the bottom half and cut the whole into pieces.

❷ In a large saucepan, bring 1 litre/1¾ pints (4½ cups) salt water to the boil with the sugar and the butter. Add the asparagus and simmer gently for 15 to 20 minutes.

❸ Remove the pan from heat and purée the soup. Mix the cornflour (corn starch) with some cream and stir it into the soup with a balloon whisk. Briefly bring to the boil again.

❹ Add the rest of the cream and season the soup with salt, pepper and the zest and juice of the lemon. Wash the parsley, chop the leaves finely and sprinkle over the soup.

Serves 4. About 190 kcal per serving

1 kg/2 lb fresh green asparagus

salt

1 teaspoon sugar

1 teaspoon butter

2 tablespoons cornflour (corn starch)

200 ml/7 fl oz (⅞ cup) cream

freshly ground white pepper

zest and juice of 1 unsprayed lemon

1 bunch parsley

Lentil soup

By adding more hot sausages to the soup and serving it with hearty slices of brown bread, you can serve it as a main course. Dried lentils must be soaked overnight and they need about 1 hour cooking time to be cooked properly. If you use lentils from a tin, the cooking time is reduced to 10 minutes.

❶ Wash the lentils and soak overnight in 1 litre/1¾ pints (4½ cups) cold water.

❷ Peel and chop the onion and the garlic finely. Wash the leek carefully and cut it into fine rings. Peel and dice the potatoes.

❸ Add the vegetables and potatoes to the lentils and slowly bring to the boil in the soaking water. Simmer for 1 hour with the lid on. If the soup becomes too thick, add more water.

❹ Add salt, pepper and marjoram to taste, put in the sausages and steam for 10 minutes with the lid on. Ladle the soup onto four large soup plates, lay a sausage on each one and serve immediately.

Serves 4. About 200 kcal per serving

250 g/8 oz lentils

1 onion

1 clove of garlic

1 leek

250 g/8 oz potatoes

salt

pepper

marjoram

4 frankfurter sausages

Pumpkin soup

In the autumn markets, pumpkins glow orange in all sizes from enormous to the small and handy. The most aromatic are the musk pumpkins or the little Hokaidos. This versatile vegetable is easy to keep all winter and it is used here in a sweet soup which will also be popular with children.

500 g/1 lb pumpkin

500 ml/17 fl oz (2¼ cups) milk

40 g/1½ oz (⅜ cup) short-grain pudding rice

50 g/2 oz (⅜ cup) ground almonds

salt

2 tablespoons rose water

cinnamon

sugar

4 tablespoons sour cream

❶ Peel the pumpkin, scrape out the seeds and dice the flesh. Cover with 250 ml/8 fl oz (1 cup) water and cook it for 30 minutes until soft. Purée with a hand blender or in a blender.

❷ Heat the milk, add the rice and let it swell over a gentle heat. Add the puréed pumpkin.

❸ Stir in the almonds. Add salt and rose water to taste. Serve with sugar, cinnamon and a swirl of sour cream.

Serves 4. About 240 kcal per serving

Onion soup

The classic onion soup originated in the bistros of Paris and it famously warms both the heart and stomach. It has allegedly helped many over a hangover, which is why it is known as "the drinker's soup" in its city of origin. If you make a large amount, it is easy to freeze. When you come to use it, browning it under the grill takes only a matter of minutes.

500 g/1 lb onions

12 cloves garlic

40 g/1½ oz (3 tablespoons) clarified butter

1 tablespoon sugar

1 sprig thyme

200 ml/7 fl oz (⅞ cup) dry white wine

750 ml/1¼ pints (3½ cups) beef stock (broth)

8 slices baguette

salt

freshly ground pepper

120 g/4 oz (1 cup) grated hard cheese

❶ Peel the onions and garlic. Cut the onions into rings and crush the garlic. Sweat in the clarified butter for about 5 minutes while stirring, but do not allow to brown. Add the sugar and thyme and pour in the wine and stock (broth).

❷ Simmer over a gentle heat for about 20 minutes. Meanwhile, toast the slices of baguette under the grill. Season the soup with salt and pepper to taste. Remove the sprig of thyme .

❸ Pour the soup into oven-proof soup bowls, not quite filling them, put two slices of toasted baguette on each one and sprinkle with cheese.

❹ Grill (broil), or bake at 200°C (400°F), Gas Mark 6.

Serves 4. About 410 kcal per serving

Brown potato soup

Potato soup is very popular and there are countless versions of it. For the typical potato taste, it is important to use a good variety of potato. In this old recipe, the soup has a nice dark colour because all the ingredients are evenly browned.

500 g/1 lb floury potatoes

¼ celeriac

1 parsnip

1 small onion

50 g/2 oz (4 tablespoons) clarified butter

1 litre/1¾ pints (4½ cups) vegetable stock (broth)

1 bay leaf

100 g/3½ oz crème fraîche

salt

freshly ground pepper

2 tablespoons chopped parsley

❶ Scrub the potatoes under running water, peel and dice. Peel the vegetables and onion. Cut them up small. Melt the clarified butter and brown the vegetables, onion and potatoes evenly over a medium heat.

❷ Add the stock (broth). Scrape the bottom of the saucepan with a wooden spoon to free any browned material, add the bay leaf, cover and cook for 40 minutes.

❸ Purée the soup with a hand blender or in a blender and stir in the crème fraîche. Season with salt and pepper to taste. Sprinkle with parsley before serving.

Serves 4. About 310 kcal per serving

Potato soup with onion rings and bacon

This spicy soup is distinctive because of its crisp onion rings and bacon. Try it hot with chili peppers, red sweet (bell) peppers and corn. Combined with the potatoes, this makes a particularly nutritious version.

❶ Wash and peel the potatoes. Wash the vegetables. Dice everything.

❷ Brown the diced vegetables briefly and add stock (broth). Simmer gently for 30 minutes. Add salt, pepper and marjoram to taste.

❸ Peel the onions and cut them into thin rings. Mix with the paprika and the flour in a bowl. Heat the clarified butter in a non-stick pan and fry the onion rings to a golden brown. Lay on kitchen paper and set aside.

❹ Cut the bacon into small cubes and fry in clarified butter until crisp. Also drain on kitchen paper.

❺ Pour the soup into soup plates and serve sprinkled with the onion rings, pieces of bacon and parsley.

Serves 4. About 270 kcal per serving

300 g/10 oz floury potatoes

2 carrots

1 small leek

1 parsnip

1 litre/1¾ pints (4½ cups) stock (broth)

salt

freshly ground pepper

1 tablespoon chopped marjoram

2 small onions

1 teaspoon sweet paprika powder

1 teaspoon plain (all purpose) flour

2 tablespoons clarified butter

200 g/7 oz bacon

1 tablespoon chopped parsley

Potato and buttermilk soup

This is a mild soup that is quickly made and has endless variations depending on what you serve it with. Croutons, sautéed courgette (zucchini) slices or browned cubes of ham are just some of the possibilities.

1 litre/1¾ pints (4½ cups) buttermilk

2 tablespoons plain (all purpose) flour

250 g/8 oz floury potatoes

salt

pepper

2 spring onions (scallions)

1 tablespoon butter

200 g/7 oz cooked ham

several sprigs chervil

❶ Put the buttermilk in a saucepan, stir in the flour with a balloon whisk and bring to the boil.

❷ Peel the potatoes and cut into small pieces. Simmer in the buttermilk for 20 minutes until they are soft. Add salt and pepper to taste.

❸ Wash and prepare the spring onions (scallions), cut into fine rings. Heat butter in a pan and cook the onions over a low heat. Finely dice the ham and add to the pan, browning for several minutes.

❹ Wash the chervil and chop fine. Ladle the soup into soup plates, add the fried ham and onions and sprinkle chervil on top.

Serves 4. About 240 kcal per serving

Celeriac cream soup

The pleasant taste of celeriac makes an excellent soup.
White wine emphasizes the delicate flavour, and the
addition of celery stalks gives it a refreshing character.

❶ Peel and wash the celeriac and cut into small dice. Melt the butter in a
saucepan and sauté the celeriac until it is golden brown. Dust with flour
and brown.

❷ Add milk to the pan, stir carefully and gradually add the vegetable
stock (broth) and the white wine. Simmer over a low heat for 30 minutes
and purée with a hand blender.

❸ Add salt, pepper and grated nutmeg to the soup to taste. Cut the
celery stalks into fine slices, heat the tablespoon of butter in a small pan
and sweat the celery in it for 5 to 10 minutes. It should still have "bite".

❹ Ladle the soup into four soup plates and add the celery. Serve with
fresh brown bread.

Serves 4. About 240 kcal per serving

1 large celeriac

50 g/2 oz (¼ cup) butter

60 g/2¼ oz (¾ cup) plain (all
   purpose) flour

500 ml/17 fl oz (2¼ cups) milk

500 ml/17 fl oz (2¼ cups)
   vegetable stock (broth)

125 ml/4 fl oz (½ cup) white wine

salt

pepper

nutmeg

2 sticks (stalks) celery

1 tablespoon butter for cooking
   the celery

Sweet (bell) pepper soup

Ripe sweet (bell) peppers give this red, creamy soup a fruity flavor, while oregano, garlic and freshly milled coloured pepper round off the taste to perfection.

5 red sweet (bell) peppers

1 hot red chili pepper

1 tablespoon olive oil

2 cloves garlic

2 onions

5 tomatoes

1 litre/1¾ pints (4½ cups) vegetable stock (broth)

salt

coarsely ground coloured pepper

fresh oregano

❶ Wash and quarter the peppers, remove the white pith and seeds and put skin side up on a grill rack. Cook for 10 to 15 minutes at 200°C (400°F), Gas Mark 6, until the skin shows signs of blistering. Remove from the oven, put in a plastic bag and seal it, then leave for 5 minutes. Take out again and peel. Set aside.

❷ Wash the chili pepper and cut into fine rings. Heat the olive oil and sweat the pepper over a low heat. Peel and finely chop the garlic and the onions, add to the chili pepper and sauté until transparent.

❸ Pour boiling water over the tomatoes and peel them. Chop and add to the onions and chili pepper. Simmer for about 5 minutes until soft,then add the bell peppers. Purée.

❹ Put the tomato and pepper sauce in a large saucepan, add the vegetable stock (broth) and cook over a low heat for 5 minutes. Add salt and pepper. Sprinkle finely chopped oregano over the soup to taste. Serve with fresh white bread.

Serves 4. About 70 kcal per serving

Cabbage soup

Cabbage and potatoes make a hearty soup that can stand in for a stew if smoked sausage is added. Leave yourself enough time to cook this soup, about 1½ hours, since the cabbage has to cook slowly.

1 kg/2 lb cabbage

500 g/1 lb potatoes

1 kohlrabi

1 onion

1 tablespoon butter

2 litres/3½ pints (9 cups) meat stock (broth)

salt

pepper

4 smoked sausages

❶ Cut the cabbage into eighths, wash it and remove the stalk and outer leaves. Cut again lengthways once or twice. Peel the potatoes and kohlrabi and cut into dice of about 3 cm/1¼ in.

❷ Peel the onions and chop very fine. Melt butter in a large saucepan and cook the onions gently until they are golden brown. Add the potatoes, cabbage and kohlrabi, pour the meat stock (broth) over and simmer on a gentle heat for 1½ hours with the lid on.

❸ Add salt and pepper to taste, cut the sausages into slices, add to the soup and cook for 10 minutes. Ladle the soup with the sliced sausage into four large soup plates and serve with thick brown bread.

Serves 4. About 320 kcal per serving

Salsify soup

This delicious root vegetable tastes similar to asparagus and is rich in protein. It is advisable to peel the salsify roots under running water since they secrete a sticky substance.

❶ Mix vinegar with 1 litre/1¾ pints (4½ cups) cold water in a bowl. Peel the salsify and immediately put in the vinegar water so that it does not discolour.

❷ Peel and chop the shallots and cut half the salsify into slices. Heat the oil in a pan and cook the shallots until they become transparent. Add the salsify and sweat briefly.

❸ Add the stock (broth), bring to the boil and simmer for 15 minutes until the salsify is tender. Purée. Beat together the egg yolk and the cream. Set aside.

❹ Meanwhile, melt the butter in a small pan, cut the rest of the salsify into 3 cm/1¼ in pieces and sauté in the sizzling butter until they are golden brown.

❺ Remove the soup from the heat and thicken with the egg and cream mixture. Do not allow to boil again. Add salt and pepper to taste.

❻ Ladle the soup into soup plates and garnish with the sautéed pieces of salsify and the chopped chives.

Serves 4. About 270 kcal per serving

100 ml/3½ fl oz (½ cup) vinegar

500 g/1 lb salsify

2 shallots

2 tablespoons oil

750 ml/1¼ pints (3½ cups) beef stock (broth)

125 ml/4 fl oz (½ cup) cream

3 egg yolks

1 tablespoon butter

salt

freshly ground white pepper

2 tablespoons chopped chives

Artichoke soup

Artichoke soup goes perfectly with an Italian menu. If you cannot find any fresh artichokes, the marinated kind will do as well. In this case the cooking time is reduced by 10 minutes.

10 artichoke hearts

2 onions

40 g/1½ oz (3 tablespoons) butter

juice of ½ lemon

1 litre/1¾ pints (4½ cups)
   vegetable stock (broth)

salt

pepper

250 ml/8 fl oz (1 cup) cream

4 artichoke hearts for garnish

50 g/2 oz (⅜ cup) shrimps

grated parmesan

❶ Wash the artichoke hearts and cut off the hard tops. Peel and quarter the onions. Melt the butter in a large saucepan and sweat the onions.

❷ Add 10 of the artichoke hearts, sprinkle with lemon juice and cook for 5 minutes. Add the vegetable stock (broth) and simmer the soup for 20 minutes. Remove the pan from heat, purée the soup and pass it through a fine sieve.

❸ Season with salt and pepper to taste. Add the cream and bring briefly to the boil again.

❹ Arrange shrimps on the 4 reserved artichokes, sprinkle with parmesan and brown quickly under the grill. Ladle the soup into soup plates and garnish each with a shrimp "boat".

Serves 4. About 320 kcal per serving

Rhubarb soup

The sour, fruity flavour of rhubarb makes a refreshing soup that can be eaten hot or cold. Serve with rusks or toasted white bread which can be easily dipped in the soup.

500 g/1 lb rhubarb

120 g/4 oz (generous ½ cup) sugar

3 tablespoons raspberry syrup

zest and juice of ½ unsprayed lemon

2 tablespoons cornflour (corn starch)

50 g/2 oz (½ cup) hazelnuts (filberts)

rusks (zwieback crackers)

❶ Wash the rhubarb, peel and cut into 2 cm/1 in pieces. Heat 1 litre/1¾ pints (4½ cups) water in a large saucepan and add the rhubarb, sugar, raspberry syrup, lemon zest and lemon juice.

❷ Cook over a gentle heat until the rhubarb is soft. Mix the cornflour (corn starch) with 2 tablespoons of cold water and beat into the hot soup. Bring briefly to the boil until the soup thickens.

❸ Serve in shallow bowls with the rusks (zwieback crackers). Chop the hazelnuts (filberts) coarsely and sprinkle on top of the soup.

Serves 4. About 260 kcal per serving

Green spring soup

This spinach soup is suitable for a light starter. In this recipe the leaves are not puréed as usual, but merely cooked quickly in the clear broth. The most suitable are the tender, small leaves of summer spinach.

1 clove of garlic

500 ml/17 fl oz (2¼ cups) beef stock (broth)

100 g/3½ oz air dried ham

100 g/3½ oz fresh leaf spinach

salt

freshly ground coloured pepper

several leaves fresh rocambole garlic

❶ Halve the clove of garlic and rub the saucepan with it. Heat the beef stock (broth) in the saucepan.

❷ Cut the ham in fine strips and set aside. Wash spinach and remove the stems. Add to the stock (broth) and allow to cook over a very gentle heat. Add salt and pepper.

❸ Wash and chop the rocambole. Ladle the soup into soup bowls, add strips of ham and rocambole and serve with a fresh baguette.

Serves 4. About 130 kcal per serving

Mediterranean vegetable soup

The charcteristic ingredients of the cuisine of the south make this soup a perfect summer meal. It should be served well-chilled with crunchy slices of baguette and a dry white wine – the one you have used for the soup would be ideal.

❶ Peel and chop the onions. Heat the oil in a large saucepan and sweat the onions until transparent. Grind the pine kernels, sea salt, sweet basil and peeled garlic with a pestle and mortar and add to the onions.

❷ Wash the courgettes (zucchini), aubergines (eggplants), sweet (bell) peppers and tomatoes and cut into 2 cm/1 in pieces. Put in the pan and sweat briefly.

❸ Put the herbs and spices in a little muslin bag (or a tea ball) and add to the vegetables in the pan. Add the white wine and simmer for 20 minutes with the lid on.

❹ Remove the bag of spices, purée the soup and pass it through a fine sieve. Add salt and freshly ground pepper to taste and set aside to cool for 2 hours.

Serves 4. About 280 kcal per serving

5 onions

4 tablespoons olive oil

50 g/2 oz (⅜ cup) pine kernels

1 teaspoon coarse sea salt

several leaves fresh sweet basil

2 cloves garlic

250 g/8 oz courgettes (zucchini)

250 g/8 oz aubergines (eggplants)

1 large red sweet (bell) pepper

250 g/8 oz tomatoes

1 bay leaf

15 peppercorns

2 sprigs fresh thyme

2 sprigs fresh rosemary

2 sprigs fresh oregano

(as an alternative to the fresh herbs, 1 tablespoon herbes de Provence)

250 ml/8 fl oz (1 cup) dry white wine

salt

freshly ground pepper

Chilled courgette (zucchini) soup

This is a light summer soup with a fine, savoury flavour that should be served chilled. Yoghurt makes the soup refreshing and easily digestible. The fragrant dill and chervil support the fairly mild flavour of the courgettes (zucchini).

2 tablespoons olive oil

2 spring onions (scallions)

2 cloves garlic

1 teaspoon coarse sea salt

2 sticks (stalks) celery

3 courgettes (zucchini)

1 tablespoon lemon juice

500 ml/17 fl oz (2¼ cups) vegetable stock (broth)

500 ml/17 fl oz (2¼ cups) low-fat yoghurt

250 ml/8 fl oz (1 cup) sour cream

½ bunch dill

½ bunch chervil

freshly ground coloured pepper

salt

1 pinch sugar

50 g/2 oz (⅜ cup) sunflower seeds

❶ Heat the olive oil in a large saucepan, clean the spring onions (scallions), cut into fine rings and sweat in the oil.

❷ Peel and quarter the garlic, and crush in a mortar with the sea salt. Add to the spring onions (scallions) and sauté gently; do not let it brown.

❸ Wash the celery and cut into thin rounds. Wash the courgettes (zucchini), cut into pieces 1 cm/½ in thick, add to pan with the celery, sprinkle the lemon juice over and steam for 3 minutes.

❹ Add the vegetable stock (broth) and simmer the soup for 5 minutes over a low heat with the lid on. Remove from heat and stir in the low-fat yoghurt and sour cream.

❺ Wash the dill and chervil, remove stalks, finely chop and stir into the soup. Add pepper and a pinch of sugar to taste and set aside to cool for 1 hour.

❻ Dry-roast the sunflower seeds, stirring them occasionally. Ladle the soup into soup plates, sprinkle with roasted sunflower seeds and serve with garlic bread.

Serves 4. About 290 kcal per serving

Chilled cucumber soup

This refreshing cucumber soup is ideal for hot summer days and should be served well-chilled. Shrimps are a perfect addition to the soup. Together with the herbs they give the soup a delicate flavour.

❶ Wash the dill and the parsley, remove the stalks and chop finely. Put the shrimps in a bowl, mix with the lemon juice and the herbs and leave in a cool place for 3 hours.

❷ Wash and peel the cucumber. Using a melon baller, scoop 16 little balls out of the cucumber flesh. Set aside to cool. Remove the seeds from the rest of the cucumber and dry with a clean tea towel or kitchen paper. Cut into small dice.

❸ Peel the onion and chop finely. Heat the vegetable stock (broth) and the white wine, add the diced cucumber and the onions and simmer over a low heat for 15 minutes until the vegetables are soft. Purée and pass through a fine sieve.

❹ Stir crème fraîche into the soup and add salt and pepper to taste. Leave the soup to cool for 1 hour, then ladle into four soup bowls. Garnish with shrimps and the little cucumber balls.

Serves 4. About 90 kcal per serving

½ **bunch parsley**

½ **bunch dill**

100 g/3½ oz (¾ cup) **shrimps**

1 tablespoon **lemon juice**

1 large **cucumber**

2 small **onions**

500 ml/17 fl oz (2¼ cups) **vegetable stock (broth)**

125 ml/4 fl oz (½ cups) **dry white wine**

2 tablespoons **crème fraîche**

salt

freshly ground white pepper

Cold summer soup

This puréed soup is deliciously refreshing on a hot summer day and awakens memories of holidays in Provence. You can also serve finely diced raw vegetables and croutons with the soup.

5 shallots

3 cloves garlic

2 small courgettes (zucchini)

1 eggplant

1 red sweet (bell) pepper

2 tomatoes

5 tablespoons olive oil

1 bay leaf

2 sprigs thyme

1 sprig rosemary

250 ml/8 fl oz (1 cup) dry white wine

250 ml/8 fl oz (1 cup) vegetable stock (broth)

salt

freshly ground pepper

1 bunch sweet basil

❶ Peel and finely dice the shallots. Peel and crush the garlic. Wash and prepare the vegetables, cutting them into small pieces.

❷ Heat the olive oil in a saucepan and sweat the shallots and garlic. Add the vegetables and brown lightly.

❸ Add all the herbs except the sweet basil and add the wine and stock (broth). Simmer gently for 20 minutes.

❹ Remove the herbs, purée the soup and pass through a sieve. Set aside to cool before serving. Wash the basil, tear the leaves into small strips and use them to garnish the soup when it is cool.

Serves 4. About 220 kcal per serving

Porcini and tortellini soup

Fresh porcini (also known as ceps, yellow boletus or Italian mushrooms) give this soup a wonderful flavour. If fresh porcini are not available, dry ones can be used instead. They must be soaked in cold water for 2 hours before cooking.

4 small firm porcini

2 shallots

1 tablespoon butter

1 litre/1¾ pints (4½ cups) beef stock (broth)

150 g/5 oz fresh tortellini, filled with cheese

1 bunch chervil

❶ Wash the porcini and cut into fine slices. Cut the slices into tiny cubes. Peel the shallots and chop small.

❷ Melt the butter in a large saucepan, cook the shallots gently until transparent, add the mushrooms and sauté.

❸ Pour in the beef stock (broth) and simmer for 2 minutes. Add the tortellini and cook in the stock (broth) for 5 minutes. They should still be firm to the bite. Wash and finely chop the chervil, adding it to the hot soup. Serve in large soup plates.

Serves 4. About 150 kcal per serving

Mushroom cream soup

Fresh mushrooms are used for this mild, creamy soup. Lots of fresh parsley, some white wine and cream make it a delight for the palate.

❶ Clean the spring onions (scallions) and cut into fine rings. Melt the butter in a large pan and sweat the onions.

❷ Rub the mushrooms with a tea towel, cut into fine slices and sweat them briefly. Dust with flour and stir in. After about 2 minutes, pour the milk over and stir in carefully to avoid lumps.

❸ Add the vegetable stock (broth) and white wine. Simmer for 15 minutes. Purée the soup. Add the cream, bring briefly to the boil again, remove from the heat and add salt, pepper and grated nutmeg to taste.

❹ Wash the parsley and chop finely. Ladle the soup into soup bowls, sprinkle with parsley and serve with croutons.

Serves 4. About 200 kcal per serving

3 spring onions (scallions)

2 tablespoons butter

250 g/8 oz fresh mushrooms

3 tablespoons plain (all purpose) flour

125 ml/4 fl oz (½ cup) milk

500 ml/17 fl oz (2¼ cups) vegetable stock (broth)

125 ml/4 fl oz (½ cup) white wine

125 ml/4 fl oz (½ cup) cream

salt

freshly ground white pepper

nutmeg

1 bunch parsley

croutons

Fish, poultry and meat soups

As well as red meat, nearly every kind of poultry is suitable for making soup. Serve duck soup (page 87) or pigeon soup (page 86) for a change to surprise your guests. Fish soups are always very delicious, such as the trout soup (page 75). For a very special occasion you could serve oyster soup (page 81) or lobster soup (page 79).

Hamburg eel soup

There are many versions of this traditional soup. In this one fresh eels are used, although it also tastes good using smoked eel. The broth can be thickened with a brown roux or with two egg yolks before being poured over the other ingredients. Semolina or other dumplings are also possible additions.

500 g/1 lb fresh eel

salt

2 carrots

¼ celeriac

1 leek

1 parsnip

1 litre/1¾ pints (4½ cups) beef stock (broth)

100 g/3½ oz green peas

2 tablespoons mixed herbs (parsley, basil, thyme, marjoram)

200 g/7 oz (1¼ cups) dried pears

200 g/7 oz (1¼ cups) prunes

250 ml/8 fl oz (1 cup) white wine

1 unsprayed lemon

1 tablespoon sugar

250 ml/8 fl oz (1 cup) wine vinegar

1 small onion, peeled and cut in half

2 cloves

1 teaspoon black peppercorns

❶ Skin the eel, clean it, cut it into pieces 5 cm/2 in long and salt it. Cover and put aside.

❷ Wash and trim the vegetables, then cut them into small pieces. Cook in the beef stock (broth) until tender, add the peas and herbs and salt to taste. Set aside.

❸ Mix the wine, zest of the lemon and sugar and cook gently together with the pears and prunes for about 15 minutes. Set aside.

❹ Put the pieces of eel in a saucepan with the spices, add 500 ml/17 fl oz (2¼ cups) water and the vinegar and bring quickly to the boil. Reduce the heat and continue to cook gently on a very low heat until done.

❺ Layer the ingredients in a tureen. Put the fruit in first, then pour over the broth with the vegetables. Lastly, arrange the pieces of eel on top.

Serves 4. About 600 kcal per serving

Trout soup

A festive soup, this could be the starter for a fish dinner. Fine strips of smoked fish are added to the mild trout soup which should be served with thinly sliced buttered toast.

❶ Wash the celery, fennel, carrots and leek and chop into small pieces. Melt the butter in a large saucepan and sauté the vegetables.

❷ Add half the washed parsley still on the stalk and sauté also. Wash the pieces of trout and add to the pan. Pour on lemon juice, white wine and 500 ml/17 fl oz (2¼ cups) water. Add peppercorns and simmer everything for 30 minutes over a gentle heat with the lid on.

❸ Strain the soup through a fine cloth to remove the fish and vegetables. Bring the stock (broth) to the boil once again and add salt and pepper to taste.

❹ Cut the smoked trout fillets into 2 cm/1 in pieces, pour the soup into small soup bowls and add the pieces of smoked trout. Wash the chives, chop and sprinkle over the soup.

Serves 4. About 150 kcal per serving

2 sticks (stalks) celery

½ fennel root

1 carrot

1 leek

2 tablespoons butter

1 bunch parsley

500 g/1 lb fresh pieces of trout (head, fins etc.)

1 tablespoon lemon juice

250 ml/8 fl oz (1 cup) dry white wine

1 teaspoon peppercorns

salt

freshly ground white pepper

2 smoked trout fillets

1 bunch chives

Fish and fennel soup

This special soup is best made with firm-fleshed fish such as halibut, cod or turbot. With its marked aromatic flavour, the fennel makes an attractive contrast to the mild fish. This soup can be part of a large menu, but it can also be served as a main course.

500 g/1 lb fish fillets

1 tablespoon lemon juice

250 ml/8 fl oz (1 cup) dry white wine

250 g/8 oz fish trimmings (heads, fins, tails)

2 shallots

2 spring onions (scallions)

1 parsnip

8 white peppercorns

1 bunch parsley

salt

freshly ground white pepper

1 fennel root

croutons

❶ Cut the fish fillets into 2 cm/1 in pieces and sprinkle with lemon juice. Set aside. Bring 500 ml/17 fl oz (2¼ cups) water and the wine to the boil, add the fish trimmings.

❷ Peel the shallots, spring onions (scallions) and parsnips, chop coarsely and add to the fish stock (broth) together with the peppercorns and parsley. Simmer the stock (broth) over a gentle heat for 30 minutes, skimming as necessary.

❸ Strain the stock (broth) through a clean cloth, and add salt and freshly milled white pepper to taste.

❹ Wash and trim the fennel. Keep the green tops for garnishing later. Remove and discard the outer leaves. Cut the rest into fine sticks. Add to the fish stock (broth) and simmer for 10 to 15 minutes until they are done.

❺ Add the pieces of fish fillet to the stock (broth) and allow to heat through gently for 5 minutes. Pour into soup plates, garnish with the green fennel tops and serve with croutons.

Serves 4. About 190 kcal per serving

Prawn (shrimp) soup

This soup can be prepared very quickly but is nevertheless a speciality that will suit a party menu. It owes its particular taste to the fact that the prawns (shrimps) are first browned.

❶ Heat the oil in a saucepan and brown the prawns (shrimps) evenly on all sides.

❷ Add the madeira and stock (broth) and simmer for 2 minutes.

❸ Whip 50 ml/2 oz (¼ cup) of the cream. Separately, beat the rest together with the egg yolks.

❹ Remove the soup from the heat and thicken with the cream and egg yolk mixture. Add salt and pepper to taste.

❺ Pour into soup bowls and garnish with a dollop of whipped cream and a sprinkling of dill.

Serves 4. About 380 kcal per serving

2 tablespoons oil

300 g/10 oz prawns (shrimps), peeled (shelled)

200 ml/7 fl oz (⅞ cup) madeira

500 ml/17 fl oz (2¼ cups) fish or chicken stock (broth)

300 ml/10 fl oz (1¾ cup) cream

2 egg yolks

salt

freshly ground white pepper

1 tablespoon dill tips

English lobster soup

In this really easy recipe the main thing is to use the best ingredients available. The flavour develops best if the soup is left in the refrigerator for 24 hours before serving.

❶ Plunge the lobster into boiling salted water, take the saucepan from the heat and leave to steep for 7 to 10 minutes.

❷ Remove the lobster from saucepan and allow to cool. Remove the meat from the claws and the shell, also remove the lobster fat and the coral. Take out the entrails from the tail and discard. Cut the flesh into bite-sized pieces.

❸ Heat the butter in a pan until it starts to sizzle. Brown the lobster fat and coral in the butter for 5 minutes. Add the pieces of lobster and simmer for another 10 minutes on a gentle heat.

❹ Add the milk gradually, stirring continuously. Let the soup to cool and put in the refrigerator for at least 12 hours.

❺ Re-heat before serving but be careful not to boil the soup again. Add salt to taste.

Serves 4. About 400 kcal per serving

2 to 3 lobsters (about 1.5 kg/3 lb in all)

salt

120 g/5 oz (⅝ cup) butter

1 litre/1¾ pints (4½ cups) fresh milk

Crab soup

There are countless recipes for crab soup. As additions, asparagus and morels harmonize well with it, although the soup is also delicious by itself with just a spoonful of cream.

500 g/1 lb crabs

salt

75 g/3 oz (6 tablespoons) butter

1 bunch of vegetables tied ready for making soup

1 onion

2 tablespoons plain (all purpose) flour

1 litre/1¾ pints (4½ cups) chicken or veal stock (broth)

20 ml/1 fl oz (2 tablespoons) cognac

1 teaspoon paprika

1 tablespoon crab butter

freshly ground white pepper

2 egg yolks

125 ml/4 fl oz (½ cup) cream

2 tablespoons chopped chives

❶ Cook the crabs in 2 litres/3½ pints (9 cups) of salted water at a rolling boil for 10 minutes, then plunge hem into cold water. Remove the meat from the pincers and tails. Set aside. Remove the entrails from the tails and discard. Crush the shells.

❷ Wash the vegetables and dice finely. Peel the onion and chop up small. Sweat the vegetables, onion and crushed crab shell in the butter. Dust with flour and add the stock (broth). Bring to the boil, then allow to simmer. After 30 minutes strain through a fine sieve and press out well.

❸ Bring the soup to the boil again and add cognac, paprika, crab butter, salt and pepper to taste. Reduce the heat so that the soup is no longer boiling. Mix the egg yolks with the cream and beat into the soup.

❹ Arrange the crab meat on four soup plates, pour over the hot soup and serve sprinkled with the chopped chives.

Serves 4. About 400 kcal per serving

Oyster soup

A delicacy for special occasions. Oysters turn this soup into a festive dish. Fish stock (broth) can be bought in delicatessens which makes the preparation less time-consuming.

❶ Open the oysters with an oyster knife, remove them from their shells and sprinkle with lemon juice. Heat fish stock (broth) and white wine together, add the oysters and cook gently for several minutes.

❷ Remove the oysters from the broth and arrange in four soup bowls. Heat the olive oil in a large saucepan, dust with cornflour (corn starch), stir and brown over a low heat. Pour on the fish stock (broth) stirring constantly and simmer for 15 minutes.

❸ Add salt, pepper and sherry to taste. Keep the soup warm on a low heat and stir in the crème fraîche. Wash the parsley and chop finely. Pour the hot soup over the oysters, sprinkle with parsley and serve with a fresh baguette.

Serves 4. About 350 kcal per serving

16 fresh oysters

2 tablespoons lemon juice

750 ml/1¼ pints (3½ cups) fish stock (broth)

250 ml/8 fl oz (1 cup) white wine

3 tablespoons olive oil

2 tablespoons cornflour (corn starch)

salt

pepper

1 tablespoon sherry

125 g/4 oz crème fraîche

1 bunch parsley

Fish roe soup

This delicious sweet and sour soup has its origin in Slav cuisine. Carp or herring roe can be used.

250 g/8 oz fish roe

1 tablespoon vinegar

500 g/1 lb pieces of fish (also heads and fins)

1 large onion

2 tablespoons butter

2 tablespoons cornflour (corn starch)

125 ml/4 fl oz (½ cup) white wine

½ teaspoon sugar

1 tablespoon lemon juice

salt

black pepper

4 slices brown bread

❶ Put the roe in a saucepan with 250 ml/8 fl oz (1 cup) water. Add vinegar and boil for 10 minutes. Strain and set the roe aside.

❷ Boil the pieces of fish in about 1 litre/1¾ pints (4½ cups) of water. Add the peeled and quartered onions and simmer for 1 hour. Strain the stock (broth) through a fine sieve.

❸ Melt the butter in a large casserole, dust with the cornflour (corn starch), add the white wine and stir briskly to avoid lumps forming. Add the fish stock (broth) and cook over gentle heat for 10 minutes.

❹ Add the fish roe to the soup and allow to heat through. Add sugar, lemon juice, salt and black pepper to taste. Serve the soup with toasted brown bread.

Serves 4. About 220 kcal per serving

Mussel soup

People who find eating mussels out of the shell too slow will enjoy this soup as a good alternative. Adding finely chopped sauerkraut to the soup makes a delicious, unusual variation.

1 kg/2 lb mussels

4 shallots

2 cloves garlic

4 tablespoons olive oil

125 ml/4 fl oz (½ cup) dry white wine

2 sprigs thyme

2 carrots

2 potatoes

750 ml/1¼ pints (3½ cups) chicken stock (broth)

juice of 1 lemon

salt

freshly ground white pepper

100 g/3½ oz crème fraîche

2 egg yolks

2 tablespoons chopped parsley

❶ Scrub the mussels thoroughly, remove the hairy beards and rinse several times. Discard any open or damaged specimens. Peel the shallots and the garlic. Dice the shallots and crush the garlic.

❷ Heat two tablespoons of oil in a saucepan and sauté the shallots and garlic until they become transparent. Add wine, thyme and mussels. Add a cup of water and simmer for 10 minutes in a saucepan with the lid on until the mussels open.

❸ Remove the mussels from their shells. Save the liquor, strain it through a fine sieve, cover and set aside.

❹ Peel the carrots and potatoes and dice very finely. Heat the rest of the oil and sweat the vegetables in it. Add the cooking liquor from the mussels and the chicken stock (broth) and cook for about 10 minutes. Add the lemon juice, salt and pepper to taste. Return the mussels to the soup and heat it again.

❺ Remove soup from heat, mix the crème fraîche and egg yolks together and thicken the soup with the mixture. Serve sprinkled with parsley.

Serves 4. About 390 kcal per serving

Goose giblets soup with barley grains (groats)

This soup can be made as a main course by simply using less liquid. In this case, serve boiled potatoes as a side dish. In Pommern in northern Germany, goose giblets are prepared with dried fruit to make a sweet and sour variation.

Giblets from two geese

salt

1 bay leaf

1 teaspoon black peppercorns

1 sprig each mugwort, marjoram and parsley

1 bunch of vegetables tied ready for making soup

100 g/3½ oz (½ cup) oat or barley grains (groats)

1 apple

1 onion

vinegar

mixed and chopped herbs

❶ Wash the giblets, cover with cold water in a saucepan and bring to the boil, skimming frequently. Pour through a sieve into another saucepan after 15 minutes, wash the giblets again and put back into the saucepan. Add herbs, spices and grains (groats) and simmer for about 2 hours.

❷ Meanwhile, wash the vegetables and cut into small pieces. Peel the onion and peel and core the apple, cutting both into thin slices. Add to the soup and cook for 30 minutes.

❸ Remove the giblets from saucepan. Remove the skin from the neck and wingtips and take the meat off the bone. Cut the livers and hearts into thin slices.

❹ Add salt, pepper and vinegar to taste. Return the goose meat to the soup and serve garnished with the chopped herbs.

Serves 4. About 150 kcal per serving

2 pigeons prepared for cooking

1 bay leaf

1 teaspoon black peppercorns

1.25 litres (2¼ pints (5½ cups) chicken stock (broth)

2 carrots

¼ celeriac

1 leek

40 g/1½ oz (3 tablespoons) butter

salt

2 egg yolks

2 tablespoon chopped parsley

Pigeon consommé with vegetables

The pigeon flavour is particularly fine in this strong broth. The meat can be taken off the bone before serving in order to save your guests from having to "work" too hard. For a more filling meal, simply add cooked noodles or rice to the soup.

❶ Wash the pigeons, cover with cold water, and bring slowly to the boil in a large saucepan with the bay leaf and the peppercorns. Skim as necessary and leave to simmer uncovered for 30 to 40 minutes.

❷ Wash the vegetables, using only the white part of the leek. Cut everything into fine slices or dice evenly. Remove some of the pigeon stock (broth) and use it to cook the vegetables in a small saucepan. Be careful not to overcook them.

❸ Remove the pigeons from the saucepan, stir the butter into the stock (broth) and strain it through a fine sieve. Add the vegetables with their cooking water to the soup and add salt to taste. Cut the pigeons in half.

❹ Mix the egg yolks in a cup with some stock (broth) and beat into the soup. while it is off the boil. Arrange the pigeon halves on four soup plates, pour over the soup and serve garnished with parsley.

Serves 4. About 300 kcal per serving

Clear duck consommé with vegetables

The intense flavour of duck is an interesting alternative to the classic chicken bouillon. The vegetables look very decorative when cut into diamond or flower shapes. It is also easy to turn this into an Asian soup by the use of soy sauce, chilli peppers, fresh coriander (cilantro), bean sprouts and Chinese noodles. Adding the thinly sliced breast of the duck makes the soup more substantial.

❶ Wash the duck giblets well and put in the saucepan along with the washed and chopped vegetables, bay leaf, pepper and salt. Cover with cold water. Bring slowly to the boil, reduce the heat and simmer until liver and heart are tender. Skim frequently.

❷ Meanwhile, wash the vegetables for the soup. Cut the carrots and celeriac into decorative slices and the leek into thin rings. Cook until just still crisp in a small amount of salted water, then rinse with cold water.

❸ Remove the pieces of duck from saucepan, strain the soup through a fine sieve, add the stock (broth) cube and stir to dissolve. Skin the neck and wingtips and remove the meat. Remove the fat from the liver and heart and cut into thin slices.

❹ Heat the duck meat and vegetables briefly in the broth and serve sprinkled with chopped chives.

Serves 4. About 200 kcal per serving

500 g/1 lb duck giblets

1 bunch of vegetables tied ready for making soup

1 bay leaf

1 teaspoon black peppercorns

2 carrots

¼ celeriac

1 leek (only use the white)

salt

1 vegetable stock (broth) cube

2 tablespoons chopped chives

Chicken and herb soup

The time it takes to make a real chicken broth is always worth while, as you will see with this recipe. The chicken boiled with the aromatic herbs makes a delicious stock (broth) which can be used as the basis for various recipes.

❶ Wash the chicken and put on to boil with 1½ litres/2¾ pints (7 cups) of water. Peel the onion, stud it with the cloves and add it and the bay leaf to the chicken. Add salt, peppercorns, juniper berries, fresh oregano and lemon balm to the soup and cook for about 1 hour.

❷ Remove the chicken from the saucepan and strain the liquid through a sieve. Discard the skin, remove the meat from the carcass, cut into thin pieces and set aside.

❸ Wash the leek, celery, carrots and parsnip and cut into thin strips. Melt the butter in a large casserole and sauté the vegetables. Pour on the chicken stock (broth).

❹ Mix the cream with the cornflour (corn starch), add to soup and bring to the boil again. Stir briskly to prevent lumps forming. Add the pieces of finely cut-up chicken meat and season with salt, pepper and nutmeg to taste. Wash the parsley, chop and sprinkle it over the soup. Ladle into soup bowls and serve with toast.

Serves 4. About 220 kcal per serving

1 boiling fowl

1 onion

1 bay leaf

2 cloves

salt

8 peppercorns

5 juniper berries

several sprigs fresh oregano

several leaves lemon balm

1 leek

1 stick (stalk) celery

2 carrots

1 parsnip

2 tablespoons butter

125 ml/4 fl oz (½ cup) cream

2 tablespoons cornflour (corn starch)

pepper

nutmeg

1 bunch parsley

Clear oxtail soup

The preparation of this classic soup certainly takes some time, but the result is definitely worth the effort. It is also easy to freeze. Instead of clarifying the soup with minced (ground) beef, you can just strain the finished broth through a cheesecloth. However, it will not be quite as clear as with the other method. For the thickened version, dust the meat and the vegetables with flour and purée the broth with the vegetables before returning the cut-up meat to the saucepan.

1 kg/2 lb oxtail, cleaned and cut into 5 cm/2 in pieces

1 slice calf knuckle, about 350 g/12 oz

1 carrot

1 leek

¼ celeriac

1 parsnip

5 tablespoons oil

1 bay leaf

2 sprigs thyme

1 teaspoon black peppercorns

250 g/8 oz ground beef

4 egg whites

1 small glass dry sherry

salt

freshly ground pepper

❶ Wash the meat in cold water and dry thoroughly. Wash the vegetables and dice finely. Heat the oil in a saucepan and brown the meat evenly on all sides. Add the vegetables and brown them too.

❷ Just cover with cold water. Add the bay leaf, thyme, peppercorns and salt. Simmer over a medium heat for 2 hours with the lid partly open until the meat is very tender. Skim frequently. Remove the meat, take off the bone and cut up into small pieces. Set aside.

❸ Return the bones to soup and cook for one more hour, skimming as needed. Strain the soup through a fine sieve and de-grease it when cool. To clarify, mix the minced (ground) beef with the egg whites, stir the mixture carefully into the soup and heat slowly. Simmer for 20 minutes and then strain through a sieve lined with cheesecloth.

❹ Add sherry, salt and pepper to taste, return the cut-up meat to the soup and re-heat.

Serves 8. About 170 kcal per serving

Gaisburger beef soup

There is a complete three-course meal hidden in this recipe, including egg pasta, beef and potatoes. Legend has it that the Swabian women from the village of Gaisburg invented this stew during the Thirty Years War in the 17th century. Their menfolk were imprisoned and the women were only allowed to bring them a single pan of food, so they simply cooked everything together, making this nutritious stew

❶ Mix the flour, egg, water and salt to a smooth dough. If it is sticky add some more flour. Bring 1½ litres/2¾ pints (7 cups) of water to the boil in a large saucepan.

❷ Spread a small amount of the dough onto a small wooden chopping board and scrape strips of the pasta into the boiling water with a knife. As soon as the pasta rises to the surface, remove with a slotted spoon, rinse under cold water and wrap in a clean, damp tea towel.

❸ Put the beef on to boil in 1½ litres/2¾ pints (7 cups) litres of cold water in a large saucepan. Wash the vegetables, coarsely chop half and add to the beef, finely dice the remainder and set aside. Add the spices and some salt to the soup and simmer on a gentle heat for about 1 hour.

❹ Peel and dice the potatoes. Wash the parsley and chop finely. Remove the beef from the broth and cut into thin strips, then cover to keep warm. Strain the broth through a fine sieve, add the diced vegetables and potatoes and cook gently for 15 minutes.

❺ Peel and chop onions, then brown them in the butter. Take them out and sauté the pasta in the same butter. Season to taste with salt and ground nutmeg.

❻ Add the fried onions, pasta, strips of beef and parsley to the soup and add salt and pepper to taste. Serve the soup in a large tureen.

Serves 4. About 370 kcal per serving

For the egg pasta dough:

80 g/3 oz (scant 1 cup) plain (all purpose) flour

1 egg

250 ml/8 fl oz (1 cup) water

salt

For the soup:

500 g/1 lb rib of beef

150 g/5 oz carrots

1 leek

50 g/2 oz celeriac

2 shallots

1 parsnip

1 small kohlrabi

2 fresh sprigs thyme

3 cloves

1 bay leaf

5 juniper berries

10 peppercorns

salt

150 g/5 oz potatoes

1 onion

30 g/1 oz (2 tablespoons) butter

nutmeg

1 bunch parsley

freshly ground white pepper

Windsor soup

It is not known if this soup was really created in the English town of Windsor on the Thames, or if it has anything to do with the British Royal Family. However, it is certainly a delicacy fit for a king, since the different meats become very tender as a result of the long cooking time. It is so filling that it can substitute for a main course.

350 g/12 oz well-marbled beef

350 g/12 oz veal

1 thick slice smoked ham weighing 150 g/5 oz

1 bunch of vegetables tied ready for making soup

3 shallots

3 tablespoons oil

40 g/1½ oz (3 tablespoons) butter

40 g/1½ oz (6 tablespoons) plain (all purpose) flour

50 g/2 oz (⅜ cup) small macaroni

salt

madeira

cayenne pepper

6 tablespoons sour cream

3 tablespoons chopped chives

❶ Cut the meat into bite-sized pieces, wash the bones well and dice the ham. Wash the vegetables and cut into small pieces. Peel the shallots and dice. Heat the oil in a large saucepan and sauté everything to a light brown. Cover with about 2 litre/3½ pints (9 cups) of water.

❷ Simmer the soup without a lid over a low heat for 1½ to 2 hours until the meat is very tender.

❸ Melt the butter in a pan and sweat the flour to a light brown. Remove 500 ml/17 fl oz (2¼ cups) of broth from the soup, add to the roux and simmer for 20 minutes. Return to the soup.

❹ Meanwhile, cook the noodles in salted water according to the instructions on the packet, then plunge into cold water. Add madeira, salt and cayenne pepper to the soup to taste and serve in soup plates with the noodles, a spoonful of sour cream and a sprinkling of chives.

Serves 6. About 440 kcal per serving

Fruit and cereal soups

Originating in farmhouse kitchens, milk soups have almost been forgotten. This is undeserved, as you will find if you try the milk soup with dumplings (page 107). Cereal soups such as the hearty barley soup (page 109) are delicious, and fruit soups including the almost black elderberry soup (page 101) will also be very popular.

Plum soup

The best time for making delicious fruit soups is the autumn, when there is a glut of fresh fruit. The plums in this recipe can be replaced with bilberries (blueberries) or blackberries if desired.

500 g/1 lb plums

1 pinch of salt

1 tablespoon cornflour (corn starch)

1 teaspoon cinnamon

1 to 2 tablespoons icing (confectioner's) sugar

125 ml/4 fl oz (½ cup) yoghurt

❶ Wash and stone (pit) the plums. Heat 1 litre/1¾ pints (4½ cups) water in a large saucepan with a pinch of salt and cook the plums until soft.

❷ Mix the cornflour (corn starch) with 1 tablespoon of cold water and beat slowly into the plums. Bring briefly to the boil and reduce the heat.

❸ Add the cinnamon and sugar to the plums to taste and stir in the yoghurt. Ladle the plum soup into bowls and garnish with small macaroons or pieces of sweet biscuits.

Serves 4. About 110 kcal per serving

Chilled orange consommé

This a refreshing and somewhat surprising soup, based on an unusual combination of delicate chicken broth and fruity oranges.

500 ml/17 fl oz (2¼ cups) chicken stock (broth)

juice of 3 oranges

2 cloves

1 chilli pepper

freshly ground white pepper

salt

1 pinch ground cinnamon

1 unsprayed orange

1 sprig lemon balm

❶ Put the chicken broth, orange juice, cloves and chilli pepper in a large saucepan and bring to the boil.

❷ Allow the broth to simmer for 5 minutes over a gentle heat, then strain through a fine cloth. Season the consommé to taste with pepper, salt and a pinch of cinnamon.

❸ Set aside to cool for 3 hours. Wash the orange and cut into thin slices. Ladle the consommé into soup bowls, garnish with the orange slices and leaves of lemon balm. Serve with little choux pastry dumplings (see Additions to soup, page136).

Serves 4. About 80 kcal per serving

Sweet fruit soup

This soup, made from fresh fruit and served well chilled, gives a real dose of vitamins. You can choose the fruit according to the season and your personal taste, garnishing it with berries.

1 Peel the banana, cut into slices, put in a large bowl and immediately sprinkle with lemon juice. Peel the peach, remove the stone (pit) and cut into bite-sized pieces. Peel the mango and cut the flesh into strips. Add fruit to the bowl.

2 Peel the apple, pear and orange and remove the cores and pips (seeds). Cut into bite-sized pieces. Put in the bowl with the other fruit and mix everything together.

3 Stir the kiwi or apricot nectar into the yoghurt and sweeten with concentrated pear juice and the vanilla sugar. Add to the bowl of fruit and refrigerate for 30 minutes.

4 Spoon into bowls and garnish with raspberries and fresh mint leaves.

Serves 4. About 290 kcal per serving

2 bananas

juice of 1 lemon

1 peach

1 mango

1 apple

1 pear

1 orange

500 ml/17 fl oz (2¼ cups) low fat yoghurt

500 ml/17 fl oz (2¼ cups) kiwi or apricot nectar

2 tablespoons pear juice concentrate

1 packet vanilla sugar

100 g/3½ oz (¾ cup) raspberries

several fresh mint leaves

Gooseberry soup

There are white, green, red and yellow varieties of gooseberry. This soup can be served warm or cold. By adding smoked strips of turkey breast, it becomes an elegant starter for an Asian menu.

❶ Wash the gooseberries, remove the stalks and the little hairs.

❷ Put the sugar in a heavy pan and allow to caramelize until it is light brown. Add the gooseberries and pour the wine and apple juice over them. Stir in the curry powder and simmer covered for 10 minutes.

❸ Wash the lemon balm, chop the leaves from two of the sprigs and add to the soup. Blend the soup and pass through a sieve.

❹ Serve garnished with the remaining leaves of lemon balm.

Serves 4. About 340 kcal per serving

500 g/1 lb gooseberries

150 g/5 oz (⅔ cup sugar

250 ml/8 fl oz (1 cup) white wine

250 ml/8 fl oz (1 cup) unfiltered apple juice

1 pinch curry powder

4 sprigs lemon balm

Elderberry soup with little yeast dumplings

Juice, syrup and fried pancakes (crepes) can be made from the dark berries of this strongly scented bush. In this recipe, the sweet, yeast dumplings turn the soup into a main course.

1 Put the sugar in a heavy pan and caramelize until light brown. Add the washed berries and pour the wine ove them. Simmer for 10 minutes. Blend the berries and pass through a sieve. Mix the cornflour (corn starch) with some water and stir until smooth. Add to the soup and briefly bring to the boil again .

2 For the dumplings, sift the flour into a bowl and make a well in the centre. Heat one-third of the milk until lukewarm. Dissolve the yeast and 20 g/1 oz (1 tablespoon) sugar in the milk and add to the flour. Turn some of the flour from the edge of the well onto the surface and leave covered in a warm place for 15 minutes.

3 Knead vigorously with the egg yolks, 20 g/1 oz (1 tablespoon) sugar, half the butter, salt and lemon zest. Make the dough into little balls and leave to rise for 30 minutes.

4 Bring the remaining milk with the butter and sugar to the boil in a large saucepan. Add the little balls of dough, leaving room between them, and cook over a low heat for 20 minutes with the lid on.

5 Dust icing (confectioner's) sugar over the finished dumplings and caramelize them briefly under the grill.

6 Ladle the soup into soup plates and add the dumplings.

Serves 4. About 440 kcal per serving

For the soup:

50 g/2 oz (¼ cup) sugar

300 g/10 oz elderberries

100 ml/3½ fl oz (½ cup) red wine

2 teaspoons cornflour (corn starch)

For the dumplings:

200 g/7 oz (2 cups) plain (all purpose) flour

15 g/½ oz (1 tablespoon) yeast

250 ml/8 fl oz (1 cup) milk

60 g/2 oz (¼ cup) sugar

1 egg yolk

30 g/1 oz (2 tablespoons) butter

pinch of salt

zest of ½ unsprayed lemon

2 tablespoons icing (confectioner's) sugar

Lemon rice soup

Reminiscent of Asian cuisine, this is a very light and fragrant soup. It is made with unsprayed lemons and rice and should be served piping hot. Serve it with white bread.

1 litre/1¾ pints (4½ cups) vegetable stock (broth)

juice of 2 lemons

2 stalks lemongrass

2 spring onions (scallions)

4 tablespoons basmati rice

1 teaspoon sugar

1 tablespoon dry sherry

salt

pepper

soy sauce

zest of 1 unsprayed lemon

1 whole unsprayed lemon

several mint leaves

❶ Bring the vegetable stock (broth) and lemon juice to the boil in a large saucepan. Beat the lemongrass stalks to flatten them slightly and add to the stock (broth). Clean the spring onions (scallions), cut into fine rings and add them.

❷ Wash the rice and stir into the boiling soup. Reduce the heat and simmer for 20 minutes with the lid on. Remove the lemongrass stalks.

❸ Add sugar, sherry, salt, pepper and a dash of soy sauce for a piquant flavour. Add the lemon zest and leave the soup to steep for another 3 to 4 minutes.

❹ Wash the whole lemon and cut it into eight segments. Ladle the soup into Asian soup bowls and garnish with the lemon segments and the mint leaves.

Serves 4. About 70 kcal per serving

Sour cherry soup with semolina dumplings

The season for sour cherries is very short. Try this delicious soup in which the tangy cherry aroma combines with the mild sweetness of the semolina dumplings. If you are cooking for children, use red juice instead of the wine.

1 Wash, stone (pit) and chop the cherries. Save any juice. Set one-third aside and crush the rest.

2 Put the sugar in a heavy pan and cook to a light brown colour. Add the crushed cherries, red wine and 250 ml/8 fl oz (1 cup) water. Add the cinnamon stick and lemon peel and simmer everything over a gentle heat for 15 minutes.

3 Strain the soup through a sieve and firmly press out the juice from the cherry pulp. Stir the cornflour (corn starch) with the cherry brandy until smooth and beat into the hot soup. Add the remaining cherries and bring briefly to just below boiling point.

4 Meanwhile, boil the milk for the dumplings and add lemon zest, salt, sugar and almonds. Sprinkle in the semolina, stirring constantly, and allow to swell for 4–5 minutes, still stirring.

5 Remove from heat and fold in the egg yolks one by one. Allow to cool a little.

6 Form little dumplings with two wet spoons and cook in simmering salted water until they rise to the surface.

7 Ladle the cherry soup into shallow soup plates and add in the dumplings. Garnish with lemon balm.

Serves 4. About 500 kcal per serving

For the soup:

1 kg/2 lb sour cherries (such as morello)

100 g/3½ oz (½ cup) sugar

250 ml/8 fl oz (1 cup) dry red wine

stick of cinnamon

peel from 1 unsprayed lemon

1 tablespoon cornflour (corn starch)

40 ml/2 fl oz (4 tablespoons) cherry brandy

For the dumplings:

250 ml/8 fl oz (1 cup) milk

zest of 1 unsprayed lemon

pinch of salt

50 g/2 oz (¼ cup) sugar

30 g/1¼ oz (¼ cup) ground almonds

50 g/2 oz (⅓ cup) semolina

2 egg yolks

lemon balm

Yoghurt soup
with raspberries

In summer, a sweet soup such as this chilled one with yoghurt and raspberries is particularly refreshing. You can replace the raspberries with bilberries (blueberries) or strawberries if desired. However, you should use only one kind of berry at a time.

500 ml/17fl oz (2¼ cups) low fat yoghurt

250 g/8 oz crème fraîche

juice of 1 lemon

3 tablespoons icing (confectioner's) sugar

300 g/10 oz(2 cups) raspberries

100 ml/3½ fl oz (½ cup) cream

several mint leaves

❶ Mix the yoghurt and crème fraîche well with the lemon juice and the icing (confectioner's) sugar. Add about one-third of the raspberries and reserve the rest for garnishing.

❷ Blend the yoghurt mixture with the berries and refrigerate for 1 hour.

❸ Whip the cream. Fill cooled bowls with the yoghurt soup and decorate with the reserved raspberries. Garnish with the whipped cream and the leaves of mint.

Serves 4. About 440 kcal per serving

Plain flour soup

The simplest type of thick soup is based on the classic roux. This soup gains it's special flavour from the red wine and the parmesan.

1 onion

80 g/3 oz (6 tablespoons) butter

120 g/4 oz (generous cup) finely ground spelt (German wheat) flour

1 litre/1¾ pints (4½ cups) vegetable stock (broth)

100 ml/3½ fl oz (½ cup) red wine

salt

pepper

50 g/2 oz (⅓ cup) parmesan

❶ Peel the onion and grate finely. Melt the butter in a large pan and sweat the grated onion. Sieve the flour into the pan and brown while stirring constantly.

❷ Add the vegetable stock (broth) to the roux and beat while bringing to the boil. Reduce the heat and simmer for 30 minutes. Add the red wine. Keep the soup warm but do not let it boil again. Season to taste with salt and pepper.

❸ Ladle into soup bowls and grate the parmesan straight onto the soup. Serve with brown bread croutons.

Serves 4. About 320 kcal per serving

Milk soup

For this soup little pasta-like dumplings are made from rye flour, cheese and water, cooked in the milk. They give the soup a creamy consistency.

❶ Knead the rye flour with the grated cheese and 3 to 4 tablespoons water into a firm dough. If the dough is too crumbly, add a little more water.

❷ Refrigerate the dough for 15 minutes, then roll it out on a wooden board and cut into short noodles with a knife.

❸ Bring the milk, buttermilk and salt to the boil, add the noodles and leave to steep over low heat for 5 minutes until they are done. Add salt, pepper and grated nutmeg to the milk soup to taste.

Serves 4. About 160 kcal per serving

70 g/3 oz (¾ cup) rye flour

50 g/2 oz (½ cup) grated Emmental cheese

500 ml/17 fl oz (2¼ cups) milk

500 ml/17 fl oz (2¼ cups) buttermilk

salt

freshly ground white pepper

nutmeg

Semolina soup

Semolina soup has a mild flavour and can easily be given that extra something by adding finely cut vegetables. The semolina is browned briefly in butter before being added to the soup.

❶ Melt the butter in a pan and cook the semolina to a golden brown. Bring the vegetable stock (broth) to the boil in a large saucepan, .

❷ Wash and prepare the vegetables and cut into thin strips. Add to the stock (broth) and cook for 20 minutes.

❸ Add the cooked semolina to the soup and leave it to swell for about 10 minutes. Add salt, pepper and grated nutmeg to taste. Wash the parsley, remove stalks, chop the leaves finely and add to the soup. Ladle the hot soup into soup plates and serve with toasted white bread.

Serves 4. About 160 kcal per serving

40 g/1½ oz (3 tablespoons) butter

75 g/3 oz (½ cup) semolina

1 litre/1¾ pints (4½ cups) vegetable stock (broth)

1 carrot

1 small onion

1 leek

1 small piece of celeriac

salt

pepper

nutmeg

1 small bunch parsley

Rolled barley soup

Barley is one of the oldest grains (groats) known to mankind. It contains many vitamins and trace minerals and can be used in both sweet and savoury dishes. A nutritious soup is quickly made using rolled barley.

❶ Heat the vegetable stock (broth) in a large saucepan. Sprinkle in the rolled barley, reduce the heat and simmer for 30 minutes.

❷ Add salt, pepper and grated nutmeg to taste. Continue to simmer. Mix the egg yolk and sour cream and stir slowly into the soup with a balloon whisk.

❸ Wash the chives and chop finely. Ladle the barley soup into soup bowls and garnish with the chives.

Serves 4. About 430 kcal per serving

500 ml/17 fl oz (2¼ cups) vegetable stock (broth)

6 tablespoons rolled barley

salt

pepper

nutmeg

1 egg yolk

125 ml/4 fl oz (½ cup)/4 oz (1 cup) sour cream

1 bunch chives

Bread soup

Delicious soups can be made using bread from the day before. No-one would think that they are made from leftovers. There are many variations; in this Bavarian version, fried onion rings give the soup a hearty flavour.

❶ Peel the onions and cut into fine rings. Melt the butter in a pan and fry the onions slowly to a golden brown.

❷ Arrange the onion rings on the bread slices and sprinkle on the grated cheese. Put in the oven for 5 minutes at 180°C (350°F), Gas Mark 4, to melt the cheese. Bring the meat stock (broth) to the boil.

❸ Lay the bread with the melted cheese in soup plates. Pour in the soup slowly from the edge so that the slices are barely covered and soak up the broth slowly from underneath.

❹ Wash the chives and chop into little rings. Sprinkle them over the soup with the freshly ground pepper. Add salt to taste.

Serves 4. About 260 kcal per serving

2 onions

3 tablespoons butter

4 slices stale black bread

100 g/3½ oz (1 cup) finely grated Emmental cheese

1 litre/1¾ pints (4½ cups) meat stock (broth)

freshly ground white pepper

½ bunch chives

salt

Barley soup

Barley has sadly become largely forgotten today. The husked, polished kernels are easily digestible, particularly in the form of pearl barley.

❶ Rinse the barley in cold water and put in a saucepan with the pork. Cover with the beef stock (broth) and bring slowly to the boil. Allow to swell over gentle heat for 1 hour. Remove the pork.

❷ Meanwhile, wash the vegetables and cut into small dice. Heat oil and brown the vegetables briefly. Add to the soup and cook until still crisp.

❸ Remove the rind from the piece of pork, cut the pork into small pieces and return to the soup.

❹ Season with salt and pepper and serve sprinkled with parsley.

Serves 4. About 110 kcal per serving

100 g/3½ oz (½ cup) pearl barley

250 g/8 oz piece smoked belly of pork

1 litre/1¾ pints (4½ cups) beef stock (broth)

1 carrot

1 leek

1 onion

1 large floury potato

2 tablespoons oil

salt

freshly ground pepper

2 tablespoons chopped parsley

Oat flour soup

This is a sweet, light-coloured soup that can be made fancier with fruit and nuts. The basis is a white roux made with oat flour which gives it a nutty flavour.

2 tablespoons butter

60 g/2 oz (½ cup) finely ground oat flour

500 ml/17 fl oz (2¼ cups) milk

1 pinch salt

1 tablespoon vanilla sugar

50 g/2 oz (scant ½ cup) icing (confectioner's) sugar

50 g/2 oz (⅜ cup) almonds

50 g/2 oz (⅓ cup) dried fruit such as prunes and apricots

❶ Melt the butter in a large saucepan. Add the oat flour and brown while stirring constantly.

❷ Add the milk and 500 ml/17 fl oz (2¼ cups) water to the roux and beat briskly. Cook over a medium heat for 10 to 15 minutes.

❸ Add the salt, vanilla sugar and icing (confectioner's) sugar to the oat soup to taste. Finely chop the almonds and stir into the soup. Add the dried fruit and cook gently in the simmering soup for another couple of minutes.

Serves 4. About 310 kcal per serving

Green spelt soup

Green spelt is unripe spelt, or German wheat, roasted to enhance its savoury, nutty flavour. It is an excellent basis for soups. It is usually sold as whole grain (groats), but you can sometimes buy it as wholemeal (wholewheat) flour in health food shops.

1 Mix the green spelt flour with 3 tablespoons of cold milk.

2 Heat the vegetable stock (broth) and gradually add the mixture of flour and milk. Mix it in carefully with a balloon whisk. Simmer on a gentle heat with the lid on for 25 minutes.

3 Beat the egg yolk with the cream and stir it into the soup. Do not let it boil again. Season with salt and pepper.

Serves 4. About 160 kcal per serving

75 g/3 oz (½ cup) green spelt flour

3 tablespoons milk

1 litre/1¾ pints (4½ cups) vegetable stock (broth)

1 egg yolk

125 ml/4 fl oz (½ cup) cream

salt

pepper

Beer soup

This soup is an unusual combination of dark beer, milk and exotic spices, with an especially delicate flavour. It can also be served with egg white dumplings as an addition.

500 ml/17 fl oz (2¼ cups) milk

50 g/2 oz (¼ cup) sugar

juice and zest of 1 unsprayed lemon

2 tablespoons cornflour (corn starch)

1 egg white

½ teaspoon cinnamon

nutmeg

500 ml/17 fl oz (2¼ cups) dark beer

2 egg whites

1 tablespoon vanilla sugar

❶ Bring the milk, sugar, lemon juice and lemon zest to the boil in a large saucepan.

❷ Mix the cornflour (corn starch) with the egg yolk, add to the boiling milk and stir it in, beating constantly. Allow to boil briefly.

❸ Add the cinnamon, some grated nutmeg and the beer. Re-heat the soup over a gentle heat but do not boil again.

❹ Beat the egg whites with the vanilla sugar until they are stiff. Ladle the soup into soup plates, scoop up spoonfuls of the egg white mixture and slide them into the soup. Sprinkle cinnamon on top to taste.

Serves 4. About 200 kcal per serving

White wine soup

This is an elegant soup that can be served as a dessert. It is particularly welcome on a cold winter afternoon, because the spices are reminiscent of Christmas baking.

❶ Melt the butter in a large saucepan, sprinkle in the cornflour (corn starch) and brown it lightly. Pour the white wine onto this roux and beat in carefully. Gradually add 500 ml/17 fl oz (2¼ cups) water and bring slowly to the boil.

❷ Add the sugar, vanilla sugar, lemon zest, cloves, cinnamon stick and cardamom to the saucepan and simmer everything for 20 minutes.

❸ Strain the wine soup through a fine sieve to remove the spices. Beat the egg yolk in another large saucepan and gradually add the wine soup. Bring slowly to the boil over a gentle heat while stirring constantly to a creamy consistency. Ladle into small bowls and serve with butter biscuits.

Serves 4. About 370 kcal per serving

1 tablespoon butter

2 tablespoons cornflour (corn starch)

1 litre/1¾ pints (4½ cups) fruity white wine

150 g/5 oz (¾ cup) sugar

1 teaspoon vanilla sugar

zest from 1 unsprayed lemon

4 cloves

1 cinnamon stick

pinch of cardamom

6 egg yolks

KRAW-THIP BRAND
COCONUT MILK EXTRAC
NƯỚC CỐT DỪA
EXTRAIT DE LAIT DE COCO

Soups from around the world

Soups are made in every part of the world and some are so famous that they have become celebrated far beyond the borders of their country of origin. Hungarian goulash (page 133) is a typical example. Also very popular as a first course or even as a main meal are soups based on the French bouillabaisse (page 118), which is almost a stew, and the Russian bortsch (page 128), made from many different vegetables.

Bouillabaisse

This famous fish soup from Marseilles was originally made by fisherman after they had returned with their catch, using shellfish, small shrimps and a variety of Mediterranean fish. When buying fish for your own version of this dish, ask for advice from your local fishmonger. It can be served with garlic mayonnaise (aioli) and croutons.

2 kg/4 lb mixed fish and shellfish

2 carrots

1 leek

500 g/1 lb tomatoes

2 shallots

5 cloves garlic

80 ml/3 oz (⅜ cup) olive oil

500 ml/17 fl oz (2¼ cups) dry white wine

2 sprigs thyme

1 sprig rosemary

½ bunch parsley

1 bayleaf

salt

freshly ground pepper

peel of 1 unsprayed orange

1 fennel root

2 teaspoons saffron

❶ Ask the fishmonger to gut and fillet the fish. Retain the bones and heads. Cut the larger fish into pieces.

❷ Wash all the vegetables, apart from the fennel, and cut into large pieces. Heat 50 ml/2 oz (5 tablespoons) of oil in a large saucepan, briefly fry the fish trimmings on a medium heat, then add the vegetables and brown lightly for about 5 minutes.

❸ Pour in the wine and 1 litre/1¾ pints (4½ cups) of water, add the herbs, salt, pepper and orange peel and simmer gently for about 25 minutes. If necessary, skim from time to time.

❹ Remove the vegetables, sieve the soup through a cloth, then return the vegetables and blend it.

❺ Wash the fennel, cut into quarters, then slice thinly, reserving the leafy green bits. Heat the remaining olive oil in a pan and sauté the fennel for about 5 minutes. Add the fish stock (broth) and saffron and bring everything to the boil.

❻ Add the fish. According to the size of the fish pieces, allow 5–10 minutes cooking time. Taste the soup. Adjust seasoning if necessary.

❼ Either arrange the fish on a plate and serve the soup separately, garnished with the green of the fennel, or serve all together in a large flat dish.

Serves 6-8. About 360 kcal per serving

Styrian stew with root vegetables

This delicious stew comes from Styria in Austria. It is made by slowly braising veal knuckles with root vegetables. The result is a very satisfying main course when served with potatoes.

❶ Clean and peel the vegetables as necessary and slice into thin julienne strips. Peel the shallots and cut into eighths. Heat the beef stock (broth) in a large saucepan, add the vegetables and boil for several minutes. The julienne vegetables should remain slightly firm to the bite.

❷ Remove the vegetables with a draining spoon and place on one side. Season the stock (broth) with the vinegar, sugar, salt, bayleaf, peppercorns and juniper berries. Add the veal knuckles and braise in the stock (broth) for about 1½ hours.

❸ Remove the meat from the stock (broth), cut it into pieces and serve on large soup plates. Sieve the stock (broth) through a cloth and then add the julienne vegetables to it.

❹ Pour the stock (broth) with the vegetables over the meat. Peel and grate the horseradish, wash and chop the chives and sprinkle both over the soup.

Serves 4. About 300 kcal per serving

2 celery stalks

1 small celeriac

2 carrots

2 large salsify

2 shallots

1.5 litres/2¾ pints (7 cups) beef stock (broth)

3 tablespoons white wine vinegar

1 teaspoon sugar

salt

1 bayleaf

5 black peppercorns

5 juniper berries

2 knuckles of veal

1 fresh horseradish root

bunch chives

Manhattan clam chowder

The renowned chowder clams are enjoyed all along the east coast of America. This recipe arrived with the early Italian immigrants to New York. In New England there is a version made with milk and cream. Baby clams may be used instead of chowder clams.

❶ Scrub the clams thoroughly under cold running water, leave to soak for 30 minutes and then clean and drain. Bring 500 ml/17 fl oz (2¼ cups) of water to the boil in a covered pan. Reduce the heat and cook the clams for about 5 minutes until they open. Remove any unopened shells and throw them away, since they are inedible. Remove the clams from their shells. Strain the cooking water through a cloth and add more water to make up to 750 ml/1¼ pints (3½ cups). Chop the clams and put to one side.

❷ Chop the onions and bacon finely. Clean the celery and carrots and cut into thin slices. Dice the tomatoes.

❸ Fry the bacon on a medium heat until crisp, then remove. Sweat the onions in the pan for about 5 minutes or until translucent. Add the rest of the vegetables and the cooking water from the clams. Add the thyme, bayleaf, salt and pepper and simmer for 30 minutes.

❹ Meanwhile, peel the potatoes and cut into cubes of 1 cm/½ in. Add them to the soup and cook for a further 15–20 minutes. Finally add the chopped clams to warm through. Season with salt, pepper and Tabasco just before serving.

Serves 4. About 160 kcal per serving

24 chowder or baby clams
150 g/5 oz bacon
1 onion
1 celery stalk
2 carrots
1 tin tomatoes (800 g/28 oz)
2 sprigs thyme
1 bayleaf
salt
freshly ground pepper
1 large potato
Tabasco

Minestrone

Every Italian housewife has her own recipe for minestrone. The main ingredients in this traditional soup consist of a variety of vegetables, pulses, tomatoes and rice or pasta. The soup develops even more taste when reheated. It's also well worth trying out chilled minestrone in summer.

200 g/7 oz (1¼ cups) dried beans

100 g/3½ oz belly of pork

1 onion

2 cloves garlic

2 carrots

3 celery sticks (stalks)

2 courgettes (zucchini)

1 leek

2 potatoes

3 large tomatoes

2 tablespoons olive oil

2 litres/3½ pints (9 cups) of beef stock (broth)

1 bayleaf

2 sprigs thyme

freshly ground pepper

salt

125 g/4 oz durum wheat small noodles

6 tablespoons grated parmesan

3 tablespoons chopped parsley

❶ Soak the beans overnight in cold water, then drain and leave to dry.

❷ Dice the bacon. Peel the onion and garlic, chopping the onion finely and pressing the garlic. Peel the carrots, wash the celery, and cut both into slices. Wash and dice the courgette (zucchini). Wash the leek and cut into rings. Peel the potatoes and cut into cubes of 1 cm/½ in. Pour boiling water over the tomatoes, then peel, remove seeds and chop.

❸ Heat the olive oil in a pan and cook the bacon. Add the onion and garlic and fry until transparent. Add the beans and all the remaining vegetables except for the tomatoes and simmer briefly.

❹ Add the tomatoes and stock (broth), together with the herbs. Simmer gently on a low heat for about 2 hours. Add the pasta towards the end of the cooking time, according to the instructions on the packet.

❺ Season the soup to taste and serve sprinkled with parmesan and parsley.

Serves 6. About 420 kcal per serving

Tyrolean bacon dumpling soup

This soup is filling and can be served on its own as a light lunch. The bacon gives the dumplings a strong flavour. If a milder flavour is wanted, cooked ham can be used instead of the bacon.

4 thick slices of a white loaf (at least a day old)

2 onions

50 g/2 oz smoked bacon

½ tablespoon butter

1 egg

125 ml/4 fl oz (½ cup) cream

salt

pepper

1 tablespoon flour

2 tablespoons chopped parsley

breadcrumbs

1.5 litres/2¾ pints (7 cups) meat stock (broth)

❶ Cut the stale bread into large cubes of about 2 cm/1 in. Peel and chop the onion finely. Cut the bacon into small pieces. Melt the butter in a large saucepan and, fry the onions and bacon until golden brown.

❷ Add the bread and fry briefly. Put the contents of the pan in a bowl and allow to cool. Meanwhile beat the egg with the cream and season with salt and pepper. Pour the egg mixture over the bread cubes and allow them to soak it up.

❸ Add the flour and parsley and knead the mixture well by hand. If the consistency seems too soft, add some breadcrumbs.

❹ Heat the stock (broth). With cool, moist hands form the dough into dumplings with a diameter of about 7 cm/3 in and lower them carefullly into the stock (broth). Simmer gently for about 10 minutes until they rise to the surface.

Serves 4. About 350 kcal per serving

South Tyrolean chestnut soup

The South Tyrol is celebrated for the plentiful harvest of nuts from its sweet chestnut trees each autumn. This has given rise to many local dishes in which the nutritious sweet chestnut plays an important role.

❶ Cut a cross in the top of each chestnut with a sharp knife and put them on a baking sheet. Bake in a preheated oven at 200°C (400°F), Gas Mark 6, for about 15 minutes until the skins splits open.

❷ Peel the hot chestnuts immediately. Heat the stock (broth), add the chestnuts and simmer for 15 minutes. Blend the chestnuts and stock (broth) with a hand blender, then add the white wine and salt and pepper.

❸ Add the cream to the soup and bring quickly to the boil. Remove the soup from the heat. Wash the chervil and chop finely before stirring it in. Pour the chestnut soup into soup bowls and decorate with croutons.

Serves 4. About 240 kcal per serving

300 g/10 oz sweet chestnuts

1 litre/1¾ pints (4½ cups) vegetable stock (broth)

125 ml/4 fl oz (½ cup) dry white wine

salt

freshly ground white pepper

125 ml/4 fl oz (½ cup) cream

1 bunch chervil

Zuppa Pavese (meat soup with egg and bread)

Zuppa Pavese is the Italian version of a soup which originally came from Bohemia. There are many versions of this soup, even including a sweet one made with cinnamon and vanilla sugar.

❶ Cut the stale bread into slices 1½ cm/¾ in thick and dribble a little milk over them.

❷ Put the slices of bread on a lightly greased baking sheet. Beat the eggs. Pour a little of the mixture over each piece of bread. Season with salt and pepper and sprinkle a little parmesan on top. Immediately put into an oven preheated to 200°C (400°F), Gas Mark 6, and bake for 5–10 minutes until the egg is set.

❸ Heat the meat stock (broth), pour into large soup bowls and place a slice of the baked bread in each one. Wash the chives, chop them finely and sprinkle on top.

Serves 4. About 330 kcal per serving

1 large white loaf (at least a day old)

125 ml/4 fl oz (½ cup) milk

4 eggs

salt

pepper

4 tablespoons grated parmesan

1 litre/1¾ pints (4½ cups) meat stock (broth)

1 bunch chives

fat for baking sheet

Peanut soup

The original recipe for this unusual and delicious soup comes from west Africa. Peanuts are grown there, from which a variety of sweet and savoury dishes are made. The tangy flavour of the soup comes from the use of chilli powder and lemon juice.

3 shallots

3 spring onions (scallions)

1 tablespoon butter

1 tablespoon tomato puree

chilli powder

salt

750 ml/1¼ pints (3½ cups) vegetable stock (broth)

5 tablespoons peanut butter

3 tablespoons coconut milk

freshly ground white pepper

1 tablespoon lemon juice

❶ Peel and finely chop the shallots and spring onions (scallions). Melt butter in a large casserole dish and fry the onions until lightly golden.

❷ Mix in the tomato puree and season with a little chilli and salt. Add 250 ml/8 fl oz (1 cup) of the stock (broth) and simmer for 10 minutes.

❸ Remove the soup from heat and liquidize. Add the rest of the stock (broth) and heat again gently. Gradually add the peanut butter to the hot soup with a spoon and then beat thoroughly.

❹ Finally add the coconut milk and let the soup simmer gently for a few minutes. Season with salt, freshly ground pepper and lemon juice.

Serves 4. About 200 kcal per serving

Bortsch with beef and duck

Bortsch is a rustic cabbage soup which gets its distinctive dark red colour from beetroot (beets). There are many different versions made in Russia and Poland. Depending on the size of one's purse, one can use bacon or choose a more extravagant version using beef and duck, which was originally prepared for the Russian tsars. If the preparation of the beetroot (beets) seems too much work, red wine vinegar can be used as a substitute (use a smaller amount because of its acidity).

1.5 kg/3 lb beetroot (beets)

1 teaspoon sugar

1 slice stale rye bread

750 g/1½ lb beef

2 duck breasts

2 onions

2 cloves

1 bayleaf

2 carrots

1 parsnip

1 leek

1 small white cabbage

salt

freshly ground pepper

125 ml/4 fl oz sour cream

2 tablespoons chopped parsley

2 tablespoons chopped dill

❶ To make the fermented beetroot (beets) juice, peel and grate 500 g/1 lb of beetroot into a pan. Sprinkle with the sugar and pour 1 litre/1¾ pints (4½ cups) of hot water over it. Put the bread on top, cover with a cloth and leave to stand for 3 days. Drain through a sieve. The juice will keep for several weeks in the fridge if well sealed.

❷ Wash the meat and the duck breasts, peel and halve the onions and spike with cloves. Put everything together in a pan with the bayleaf. Cover with cold water, bring to the boil and simmer in a partially covered pan for about 2½ hours. Skim the surface regularly. Remove the duck breasts after 40 minutes and put to one side, covered.

❸ Reserve two beetroots (beets) and put the rest unpeeled in a pan. Cover with water and boil until soft. Depending on the size, this will take between 1 and 2 hours. Leave to cool a little, then peel and cut into small strips. Use rubber gloves since the beetroot (beet) stains.

❹ Meanwhile, peel and wash the carrots and parsnip and cut into slices. Cut the leek into 5 cm/2 in strips. Remove the stalk and tough leaves from the cabbage and cut into small pieces. Peel and grate the two reserved beetroots (beets). Press out the juice and put it to one side.

❺ Remove the meat when tender. Put the stock (broth) through a fine sieve and remove the fat from the surface. Add 500 ml/17 fl oz (2¼ cups) of the fermented beetroot (beet) juice and the prepared raw vegetables to the stock (broth).

❻ Dice the beef, remove the skin from the duck breasts and cut into thin slices. Put them in the soup with the beetroot (beets) and the juice and heat it up. Season well with salt and pepper.

❼ Serve in deep soup bowls. Garnish with sour cream and chopped herbs.

Serves 8. About 310 kcal per serving

Sweet and sour chicken soup

There are many different recipes for chicken soup in Chinese cookery. This sweet and sour version whets the appetite and is fairly easy to prepare for special occasions. The characteristic sweet, sour and spicy flavour comes from the use of sugar, vinegar and hot sauce.

❶ Soak the mushrooms for about an hour in water. Wash the tofu (bean curd). Peel the carrots and shallots. Cut the tofu (bean curd), mushrooms, carrots and shallots into narrow strips.

❷ Cut the chicken breast into thin strips with a sharp knife. Prepare the marinade by mixing the rice wine, salt, pepper, soy sauce, ¹/₂ tablespoon cornstarch and groundnut oil. Pour this over the chicken and leave to marinate for 30 minutes.

❸ Heat the chicken stock (broth) and season to taste with tomato puree, sugar, vinegar and sambal oelek. Add the bean sprouts and carrots and simmer gently for about 5 minutes. Finally add the mushrooms, shallots and tofu (bean curd) and cook for just 3 minutes more.

❹ Mix the remaining cornflour (corn starch) with 2 tablespoons of cold water and add gradually to the soup while stirring. Bring to the boil and add the chicken.

❺ Allow time for the chicken to absorb the flavour before garnishing. Coarsely chop the watercress and garnish each soup bowl with it before serving.

Serves 4. About 130 kcal per serving

6 dried Chinese mushrooms

50 g tofu (bean curd)

2 carrots

2 shallots

300 g/10 oz chicken breast fillets

1 teaspoon rice wine

salt

freshly ground white pepper

1 teaspoon soy sauce

2 ½ tablespoons cornflour (corn starch)

1 teaspoon groundnut oil

500 ml/17 fl oz (2¼ cups) chicken stock (broth)

1 tablespoon tomato puree

1 tablespoon white wine vinegar

1 teaspoon sugar

1 teaspoon hot sauce such as sambal oelek

50 g/2 oz bean sprouts

50 g/2 oz watercress

Mongolian fire bowl

The Chinese adopted this recipe from the Mongolian nomads who settled in the north of China. The fire bowl is great fun at dinner parties and is reminiscent of the better known fondue. Wafer-thin slices of lamb as well as vegetables and noodles are immersed into the boiling stock (broth) by the guests at the table.

1 kg/2 lb lamb fillet

amounts and ingredients according to personal preference:

Chinese shi-taki mushrooms

bean sprouts

bamboo shoots

water chestnuts

carrots

red peppers

spring onions (scallions)

ginger plums marinated in honey

pickled ginger

soy sauce

chilli sauce

1 litre/1¾ pints (4½ cups) chicken stock (broth)

rice noodles

❶ Freeze the lamb briefly in the freezer to make it easier to slice. Cut into wafer-thin slices and arrange overlapping on a plate.

❷ Soak the mushrooms in cold water for 2–3 hours. Wash the fresh bean sprouts. Pat the pickles and marinated ginger plums dry with kitchen paper. Slice the water chestnuts. Peel the carrots and slice finely. Wash the peppers and cut into strips. Wash the spring onions (scallions) and cut into thick pieces. Arrange the mushrooms and vegetables in separate bowls. Also put the ginger plums, ginger and sauces in bowls.

❸ Pour the chicken stock (broth) into a fondue pan, light the burner and wait until the stock (broth) is gently simmering. Guests can prepare and cook their own selections of meat, vegetables and mushrooms using chopsticks. The guests can then dip their creations in soy or chilli sauce. The ginger and the sweet ginger plums are ideal accompaniments.

❹ Finally, the noodles can be added to the stock (broth), which by now has a rich flavour from all the ingredients cooked in it. As soon as the noodles are cooked, serve them in bowls together with the tasty stock (broth).

Serves 4. About 860 kcal per serving

Hungarian cabbage soup

Paprika, sauerkraut (pickled white cabbage) and sour cream unite harmoniously in this tasty and warming soup. It's an ideal soup for a midnight feast at a party, with finely sliced spicy sausage. The soup is best cooked a day in advance as the flavour improves when reheated. If a spicy dish is preferred, use chili pepper instead of the paprika powder.

100 g/3½ oz streaky bacon

3 floury potatoes

2 tablespoons lard (shortening)

2 onions

1 tablespoon mild paprika powder

500 g/1 lb sauerkraut

1 litre/1¾ pints (4½ cups) beef stock (broth)

6 juniper berries

1 teaspoon black peppercorns

1 bayleaf

pinch of pimento

salt

freshly ground pepper

200 ml/7 fl oz (⅞ cup) sour cream

1 bunch chives

❶ Dice the bacon finely. Heat the fat and cook the bacon.

❷ Peel the onions, dice finely and fry until translucent. Sprinkle with paprika and fry briefly. Peel the potatoes and cut into 1 cm/½ in cubes. Add to pan with the sauerkraut, then pour in the beef stock (broth).

❸ Add the herbs and simmer for about 30 minutes until the potatoes are soft. Season with salt and pepper.

❹ Wash and chop the chives. Serve the soup, garnished with sour cream and chives.

Serves 4-6. About 270 kcal per serving

Hungarian goulash soup

The most important ingredients for a Hungarian goulash soup are onions, beef and potatoes, which are slowly simmered in a fiery tomato sauce. For those who like it even hotter, it is also possible to add slices of spicy sausage at the end.

❶ Heat the lard (shortening) in a large casserole dish. Peel, finely chop and fry the onions until golden brown. Sprinkle paprika over the onions, stir and then add 4 tablespoons of stock (broth).

❷ Cut the beef into cubes and braise in the casserole. Cover the tomatoes with boiling water, then skin them and cut them into eighths, remove the seeds and add to the meat.

❸ Peel and crush the garlic cloves and add to the casserole along with the herbs and peppers. Slice the chilli peppers lengthways before adding.

❹ Pour in the remaining stock (broth) and boil gently for about 45 minutes. Peel the potatoes and carrots, chop into cubes, and add to the meat. Cook for a further 20 minutes.

❺ Remove the chilli and serve the soup in large soup plates accompanied by granary bread.

Serves 4. About 390 kcal per serving

50 g/2 oz (4 tablespoons) lard (shortening)

250 g/8 oz onions

2 tablespoons mild paprika

1.5 litres/2¾ pints (7 cups) beef stock (broth)

250 g/8 oz beef

4 tomatoes

2 cloves garlic

salt

pepper

caraway

marjoram

2 red chilli peppers (hot)

250 g/8 oz potatoes

1 carrot

Pasta e fagioli

This extremely satisfying Italian speciality is a typical dish of the poor which can also be enjoyed cold. For entertaining, crayfish tails or scampi could be added.

250 g/8 oz dried white beans

4 garlic cloves

2 bayleaves

1 sprig sage

80 ml/3 oz (⅜ cup) olive oil

100 g/3½ oz bacon

2 carrots

2 celery stalks

1 onion

1.5 litres/2¾ pints (7 cups) chicken stock (broth)

200 g/7 oz fettucine

salt

freshly ground pepper

1 sprig rosemary

2 sprigs thyme

❶ Soak the beans overnight in cold water. Peel the 2 garlic cloves and chop finely. Drain the beans, put them in a saucepan with the garlic and herbs, add 20 ml/1 oz (1 tablespoon) of the olive oil and cover with water. Bring to the boil and then simmer on a low heat for about 1½ hour until soft.

❷ Meanwhile, wash the carrots and celery, and dice into small pieces. Peel the onion and the remaining garlic cloves and chop finely. Dice the bacon. Cook the bacon in a spoonful of hot oil and then sweat the vegetables in the same saucepan. Add the stock (broth) and simmer for about an hour.

❸ Remove the bayleaves and sage from the beans. Liquidize half the beans, then add this bean puree and the rest of the beans to the vegetable stock (broth).

❹ Bring the soup to the boil, break the pasta into short pieces and cook in the soup until al dente. Season with salt and pepper.

❺ Wash the rosemary and thyme leaves, remove from the sprig and chop finely. Garnish the soup with the herbs and a few drops of olive oil.

Serves 6. About 600 kcal per serving

Gazpacho

This vegetable soup, served ice cold, is a refreshing treat on hot summer days. In Spain it is often diluted with iced water. It is served with croutons and finely chopped vegetables.

❶ Peel the cucumbers, cut in half lengthways, remove seeds and finely dice. Place the tomatoes briefly in boiling water, remove skins and seeds and tough middle and cut into eighths. Wash the peppers, remove seeds and finely dice. Peel and finely chop onion.

❷ Put three-quarters of the cucumber, onions, peppers and tomatoes in the mixer. Put the remaining vegetables to one side. Peel and finely chop the garlic and add to the vegetables in the mixer. Remove crust from the bread, dice, and then add three-quarters of that to the mixer also.

❸ Add the olive oil and vinegar and liquidize all in the mixer. Season with salt and pepper and add the tomato puree. If the consistency of the soup is too thick, add a little iced water.

❹ Cover the gazpacho and leave it to cool in the refrigerator for about 2 hours. Just before serving, beat vigorously. Fry the remaining diced bread until golden brown and serve along with the remaining vegetables in small bowls.

Serves 4. About 250 kcal per serving

2 cucumbers
500 g/1 lb tomatoes
3 onions
1 green pepper
1 red pepper
3 garlic cloves
½ white loaf
4 tablespoons olive oil
4 tablespoons red wine vinegar
Salt
Freshly ground black pepper
2 tablespoons tomato puree

Additions to soups

You can vary a basic soup by what you add to it, changing the flavour and character according to taste. You can have a light soup one day and a heartier one on another occasion. Whether you choose to add marrow dumplings (page 144), salmon dumplings (page 147), eggs (page 148), or leftover pancakes (crepes) (page 150), will depend largely on the main course. If the course that follows is fairly light, you can enjoy a more filling soup as a starter.

Bread croutons

Fried bread croutons are a perfect finishing touch for cream soups, and in fact they go well with almost every soup. They are quite filling and can turn a starter into a satisfying meal.

Fried bread cubes

Cut stale white or wholemeal (wholewheat) bread into cubes. Melt a tablespoon of butter in a large frying pan. Add the bread cubes and fry on the lowest heat until golden brown, shaking them from time to time to turn them.

Garlic croutons

Cut white bread or rolls into pieces 1 cm/½ in thick, rub the surface with half a garlic clove and fry in a little olive oil until golden brown.

Baked white bread croutons

It is quick and easy to bake a large quantity of croutons in the oven. These are perfect for hot bouillons and consommes. Cut a loaf of bread into slices 1 cm/½ in thick. Spread with a little butter, sprinkle with salt and pepper, and bake until crisp at 180°C (350°F), Gas Mark 4.

Roasted bread with cheese

The ideal accompaniment for traditional French onion soup. Slice a baguette, cover each piece with grated Emmental cheese and bake on a baking sheet at 180°C (350°F), Gas Mark 4, until the cheese has melted and the bread is crisp.

Herb bread

Slices of white bread rubbed with garlic, spread with a little butter and sprinkled with finely chopped basil or parsley are a perfect complement to a hearty Italian minestrone soup.

Mozzarella bread

A delicious addition, not only for Italian soups. Cut slices of white bread into small squares and cover each with a little mozzarella. Place 2–3 fresh oregano leaves and pepper on top and then cook in oven until the cheese melts.

Semolina dumplings

A classic Bavarian and Austrian recipe. Semolina dumpling soup is light and easy to digest. Use a home-made stock (broth) for this fine soup if possible, since it enhances the delicate flavour of the dumplings.

For 1 litre/1¾ pints (4½ cups) of beef stock (broth):

50 g/2 oz (4 tablespoons) softened butter

1 egg

2 teaspoons finely chopped chervil

salt

nutmeg

100 g/3½ oz (½ cup) durum wheat semolina

❶ Cream the softened butter in a bowl. Add the egg, chervil, salt and a pinch of grated nutmeg. Slowly pour the semolina into the mixture and stir in well. Leave for 30 minutes to let the semolina swell.

❷ Bring the beef stock (broth) slowly to simmering point. Using a teaspoon, form little oval dumplings from the mixture, smoothing them out on the edge of the bowl. Scrape off with a second teaspoon and slide carefully into the simmering stock (broth).

❸ Simmer dumplings gently for 10–15 minutes in the stock (broth) until they float to the surface. They should be soft on the outside, yet still firm on the inside.

Serves 4. About 260 kcal per serving

Choux pastry as a soup accompaniment

An original soup accompaniment for which a traditional choux pastry is required – the type which is usually made into a sweet, rather than a starter! In this case the pastry is neutral, that is to say, without sugar, and the crisp pieces taste excellent in the soup.

For 1 litre of soup:

50 g/2 oz (4 tablespoons) butter

a pinch of salt

100 g/3½ oz (1 cup) wheat flour

3 eggs

fat for the baking sheet

❶ Boil 125 ml/4 fl oz (½ cup) water with the butter and salt. Take the pan from the stove, quickly sieve in the flour and stir until smooth.

❷ Return the pan to the heat and stir well until the pastry dough falls away from the sides of the pan and forms into a large mass.

❸ Take the pan off the heat again and stir 1 egg into the hot dough. Allow the pastry to cool briefly, and then gradually add the remaining eggs. Allow to rest for 30 minutes.

❹ Grease a baking sheet, fill a piping (decorator's) bag with the dough and squeeze out small blobs onto the tray. Put the tray in the oven with a heat-resistant bowl filled with water underneath it – the steam helps the pastry dough to rise well. Bake at 200°C (400°F), Gas Mark 6, until golden brown.

Serves 4. About 240 kcal per serving

Bone marrow dumplings

In Austria it is customary to start a meal with a hearty soup, usually made from beef and bones. The marrow from the inside of the bones is a practical and tasty addition.

For 1 litre/1¾ pints (4½ cups) of stock (broth):

80 g/3 oz beef marrow

1 egg

1 egg yolk

1 tablespoon chopped parsley

nutmeg

salt

pepper

100 g/3½ oz (2 cups) fresh breadcrumbs

❶ Chop the marrow finely and render it in a pan without allowing it to brown. Scoop out some of the melted fat.

❷ Place the marrow in a mixing bowl together with the egg and egg yolk and beat until foamy. Add the parsley, pinch of nutmeg, salt and pepper and finally the breadcrumbs. If the mixture is too sticky to form into dumplings, add more breadcrumbs. Leave to cool for 20 minutes.

❸ Form the dough into small dumplings with floured hands and put them on a plate. Heat the stock (broth) to simmering point, add all the dumplings at once and allow to simmer gently for 10–15 minutes. Avoid boiling or they may fall apart.

Serves 4. About 350 kcal per serving

Homemade soup noodles

Homemade noodles are hard to beat as a delicious and very special soup accompaniment. Spelt flour (also known as German wheat flour) has a more distinctive flavour than ordinary flour and is ideal for the noodle dough. The best stock (broth) to use is either beef or chicken.

For 1 litre/1¾ pints (4½ cups) of stock (broth):

100 g/3½ oz (1 cup) finely ground spelt flour

1 egg

a pinch of salt

❶ Mix the flour, egg and pinch of salt into a smooth dough. Knead the dough until small bubbles appear on the surface when cut and the consistency is elastic.

❷ If the dough seems to be too firm, add a few tablespoons of lukewarm water. Leave to rest for 15 minutes. Sprinkle a board with flour, roll the dough out thinly and leave to dry for about 10 minutes.

❸ Cut the dough into thin strips. Gently remove the noodles from the board by hand. Put them in boiling beef or chicken stock (broth) for a few minutes. Test the noodles often to see if they are ready – homemade noodles take less time to cook than ready-made ones!

❹ Garnish the soup with finely chopped fresh herbs and add salt and pepper to taste.

Serves 4. About 170 kcal per serving

Salmon dumplings

This light addition is suitable for clear fish soups or ones made with a roux. The dumplings also taste delicious served with chervil sauce and a small salad.

❶ Rinse and dry the fish and cut it into small pieces. Peel the shallot and dice it finely. Fry the shallot briefly in hot butter without letting it colour. Add the salmon and then pour in the stock (broth) and white wine. Let it boil briefly, then remove from the pan from the heat and leave to cook through for 5 minutes.

❷ Beat the egg white with a little salt until it makes stiff peaks. Remove the salmon from the stock (broth) and blend it in the mixer. Fold it carefully into the mixture together with the flour. Season with salt, pepper and chervil. Leave the mixture to cool for 30 minutes in the fridge.

❸ Form small dumplings with a dessertspoon and poach for 5 minutes in gently simmering salted water.

Serves 4. About 190 kcal per serving

For 1 litre/1¾ pints (4½ cups) of soup:

250 g/8 oz salmon fillet

1 shallot

1 tablespoon butter

250 ml/8 fl oz (1 cup) fish stock (broth)

125 ml/4 fl oz (½ cup) dry white wine

2 egg whites

salt

1 tablespoon flour

freshly ground white pepper

1 tablespoon chopped chervil

Cheese dumplings

All kinds of soups and broths can be varied in interesting ways with additions. A quick and tasty idea is to add cheese dumplings, which are also a good way of using up leftover cheese.

For 1 litre/1¾ pints (4½ cups) of soup:

2 eggs

20 g/¾ oz (1½ tablespoons) butter

5 tablespoons grated Gruyère cheese

salt

white pepper

egg white

❶ Hard-boil the eggs, place in cold water and then shell. Mash the yolk with a fork and finely chop the egg white.

❷ Add the softened butter and grated cheese to the prepared egg and mix together carefully. Season with a little pepper and salt. If the mixture seems too dry, knead in a little runny egg white.

❸ Heat the meat stock (broth). Form little dumplings from the mixture with a teaspoon and put them in the stock (broth). Simmer the cheese dumplings gently, being careful not to let them boil.

Serves 4. About 240 kcal per serving

Egg strips

In France this accompaniment is a firm favourite for special meat soups. It is easy to make attractive shapes out of the set egg with a pastry cutter.

For 1 litre/1¾ pints (4½ cups) of soup:

2 eggs

4 tablespoons milk

1 tablespoon cream

salt

pepper

nutmeg

1 teaspoon butter

❶ Beat the eggs with the milk and cream in a bowl.

❷ Season with salt, pepper and a little grated nutmeg. Put the egg mixture in a buttered jelly mould with a smooth base. Put the mould in a bain marie and steam for about 15 minutes until the egg mixture sets.

❸ Remove the mould from water, leave to cool and ease the egg mixture out onto a flat plate. Cut it into thin strips, cubes or diamond shapes, or cut out other shapes with pastry cutters. Put in the soup plates and add hot soup.

Serves 4. About 60 kcal per serving

Pancake (crepe) soup

Pancake (crepe) soup is one of the traditional classics. The soup looks especially appetising when the pancakes (crepes) are cut into decorative shapes with pastry (cookie) cutters.

For 1 litre/1¾ pints (4½ cups) of soup:

6 heaped tablespoons flour

250 ml/8 fl oz (1 cup) milk

2 eggs

salt

1–2 tablespoons butter

❶ Put the flour into a bowl, slowly mix in the milk with a wisk, add the eggs and salt and blend until smooth. Allow the batter to rest for 30 minutes.

❷ Melt the butter in a frying pan, add 2–3 teaspoons of the batter and spread it evenly over the pan. Cook until golden on both sides. Make 4 pancakes (crepes) in this way.

❸ Lay the pancakes (crepes) on a flat plate on top of each other and cut it into patterned shapes with small pastry (cookie) cutters.

❹ Heat the meat stock (broth) and add the pancake (crepe) shapes.

Serves 4. About 220 kcal per serving

Liver dumplings

Liver dumpling soup is a classic in southern Germany, often served before the Sunday roast. This starter tastes best of all when the dumplings are left to soak for a while in the soup.

❶ Mince (grind) or chop the liver and put it in a large bowl. Soak the bread rolls in a little water, firmly squeeze out excess water by hand and add to the liver. Beat the egg and add it.

❷ Peel the onions, chop finely and lightly brown in butter. Wash the parsley, chop finely and put in the bowl with the onion and liver mixture. Add the marjoram and seasonings and knead the mixture by hand. If the mixture is too sticky, add some breadcrumbs. Leave to cool for 30 minutes.

❸ Bring the beef stock (broth) to simmering point. With cool, damp hands, form dumplings about 5 cm/2 in diameter and slide them carefully into the stock (broth). Leave the dumplings to simmer gently for 10 minutes, avoiding boiling.

Serves 4. About 300 kcal per serving

For 1 litre/1¾ pints (4½ cups) of soup:

150 g/5 oz ox liver

2 stale bread rolls

1 egg

2 onions

30 g/1 oz (2 tablespoons) butter

½ bunch parsley

salt

freshly ground black pepper

pinch grated nutmeg

1 teaspoon marjoram

breadcrumbs

Index

Produced by Meidenbauer - Martin Verlagsbüro, Munich, Germany

Editorial staff Caroline Bush, Jacqueline Lawson

Layout and typesetting Hubert Grafik Design, Munich, Germany

Photography Brigitte Sporrer and Alena Hrbkova

Food preparation Tim Landsberg

Cover design Stockfood/Schieren

Cover photograph © Stockfood/ Schieren

Translation Greta Dunn and Nina Merrens

Printed and bound by Druckerei Appl, Wemding, Germany

© 2000 DuMont Verlag, Cologne, Germany
(monte von DuMont)
All rights reserved

ISBN 3-7701-7004-0

Printed in Germany

All rights reserved. No part of this book may be reproduced, stored in a retrieval system or transmitted in any form or by any means, electronic, electrostatic, magnetic tape, mechanical, photocopying, recording or otherwise, without the prior permission in writing of the publisher.

The recipes in this book have been carefully researched and worked out. However, neither the author nor the publishers can be held liable for the contents of this book.

The editors and publishers would like to give special thanks to the following businesses for their support of this book:
Culti, Munich, Germany: 68
Rosenthal Studio-Haus, Munich, Germany: 77, 78, 88, 108, 141, 146, 152
Porzellan Manufaktur Nymphen-burg, Munich, Germany: 9

The photographers:

Brigitte Sporrer and Alena Hrbkova met each other while training as photographers in Munich, Germany. After working as assistants to various advertising and food photographers, they now each have their own studios in Munich and Prague respectively.

The food preparer:

Tim Landsberg, who learned to cook in Bonn, Germany, works in Munich as a food stylist. His customers are from the printing and television advertising branches. He also likes to work on cookbooks.